Before They Were Beatles

Before They Were Beatles

The Early Years: 1956-1960

Alan J. Porter

Copyright © 2003 by Alan J. Porter.

Library of Congress Number: 2003096630
ISBN : Hardcover 1-4134-3057-0
Softcover 1-4134-3056-2

All rights reserved. No part of this book may be reproduced or transmitted in any form or by any means, electronic or mechanical, including photocopying, recording, or by any information storage and retrieval system, without permission in writing from the copyright owner.

This book was printed in the United States of America.

To order additional copies of this book, contact:
Xlibris Corporation
1-888-795-4274
www.Xlibris.com
Orders@Xlibris.com
21351

CONTENTS

INTRODUCTION 11

PART ONE
    "And The Band Began To Play"—1956 15

PART TWO
    "Lennon & McCartney"—1957 40

PART THREE
    "Tragedy & First Recording"—1958 69

PART FOUR
    "Rockin' The Casbah"—1959 79

PART FIVE
    "Moondogs to Beatles"—1960 94

WHATEVER HAPPENED TO . . .? 124

EVOLUTION OF A BAND 131

THE MUSIC (1957-1960) 133

BIBLIOGRAPHY 141

REFERENCES 149

*For my parents, May & Derek Porter.
Thanks for planting the seed that grew into my love for music . . .*

Other Books by Alan J. Porter

"The Unauthorized BATMAN Collectors Guide"
Schiffer Books, ISBN 0764306839

Contributor to:
"MANSELL: The People's Champion"
HarperCollins, ISBN 0002184974

A full list of published works and details on new projects can be found at the author's website http://alanjporter.com

INTRODUCTION

Strawberry Fields, Central Park, New York.

It's early on a sunny September morning, the air is crisp and the squirrels are playing in the trees around me. The tourists are starting to arrive in a steady stream. Some walk over it without noticing, others stop and look as if to say "is that it?" But a few stop, bend down and touch the mosaic tiles that spell out a single word. IMAGINE. Their faces reflecting memories, hopes and dreams.

For me this is the culmination of a personal journey that began twenty years ago and an ocean away, when I first stood outside the gates of Strawberry Field in Liverpool, England. I was born and lived the first twenty years of my life on the banks of the River Mersey about 30 miles upstream from Liverpool. Shortly after my 4th birthday the family bought its first TV set.

I remember watching a Popeye cartoon followed by an early evening show, broadcast by a local station, called "Scene at 6.30". I was allowed to stay up as a treat. Something on that show caught my imagination—a strange sort of music I hadn't heard before. My parents preferred light opera to rock 'n' roll.

It was October 18th 1963 and The Beatles had entered my life. From then on I loved their music. As with all other kids of my generation I played at being "The Beatles" in the streets, complete with plastic guitars. As I grew older I discovered other bands and sounds, but underlying them all was the influence of the "Fab Four."

In the mid 70's Punk had exploded on the scene. Some friends formed a band and I ended up playing one gig (as support to The Buzzcocks) as a substitute bass player, unwittingly imitating one of the early Beatles' "back-to-the-audience" techniques to cover my lack of skill.

In the late 1970s I attended Riversdale Technical College in Liverpool, where I was surprised to learn that Richard Starkey, better known as Ringo Starr, had once, albeit briefly, been a student. I also suddenly found myself amid places with familiar names such as "Penny Lane" and "Strawberry Fields." I spent most of my time listening to local bands playing in small dank nightclubs—hearing tales of the Mersey Beat era and The Cavern club—this all lead to an interest in uncovering the early history of The Beatles.

I was determined to find out exactly what combination of circumstance, influences and even chance encounters transformed a school-boy band (one of thousands in late 1950s Britain) into the rock'n'roll group that headed to Hamburg in 1960 billing themselves under the newly acquired name of The Beatles.

And what a journey it has been! This book is the culmination of many years' research involving hundreds of books, magazines, newspapers, websites; many hours of music and a rediscovery of what made The Beatles so special. It has also opened my eyes to the pitfalls and perils that are faced by anyone who has the vague notion of writing a biography. History is fickle and memory is selective even with recent events. That has proved to be the case in nearly every aspect of the story of the Beatles' early years in Liverpool. Nobody documents the minutiae of their teenage years and we certainly don't think that the games we play and the schoolboy fantasies and attempts at defining a role for ourselves will be noteworthy to future historians. The teenagers who populate this story were no different from the rest of us. As a consequence most of the "facts" surrounding the early years of The Beatles are lost to the mists of time.

Where possible I have tried to verify facts against contemporary published resources, where they exist. Otherwise one has to rely on the memory of those who were present, both central and peripheral. Over the years that memory is subject to change, sometimes in an effort to inflate a person's own importance or to promote a particular personal agenda. Recollections are often contradictory. Often though it is no more than an inability to recall the exact circumstances or facts. While frustrating to the researcher, it is something I fully understand as I can't even recall the name of the band I played in as a teenager, it was only for one gig after all.

Within these pages I have attempted to present a near chronological story that charts the converging paths of the main players in the Beatles story between the years 1956 and 1960. Dates and events have been determined by comparing various sources, published and unpublished, and in some cases I will admit to the occasional educated "guess" as to when a particular incident fits into the time frame. Any errors or omissions are my own.

A journey like this is not made alone. I'd like to thank my wife Gill and my daughters Meggan and Erin for their unfailing support during the research and writing of this book. Marty Arnold, who not only was brave enough to try and teach me to play the bass guitar, but also shared his passion for the intricacies of The Beatles music. Kari Johnson who read an early draft of the book and pointed out all those assumptions I was making that wouldn't have meant anything to the casual reader. Mike Aragona for being a vocal supporter of this project since its inception and for his editorial insight and expertise at every stage. Gabriel Morrissette for taking my vague ideas and turning them into great cover art. And lastly I must extend a large and heartfelt thanks to Mr. Rod Davis of The Quarrymen, who was there for most of the story told in these pages and was kind enough to share his recollections.

And of course a large vote of thanks to John, Paul, George and Ringo as well as Stuart, Pete (both of them), Rod, Eric, Colin, Len, Norman, Tommy, Ken and everyone else who played a part. Without them there would be no story to tell.

Alan J. Porter—Maryland, 2003

PART ONE

"And The Band Began To Play"—1956

January 1956

The Fab Four, the lovable mop-tops, symbols of a generation, musical geniuses, the greatest composers of the age or just a simple pop group. It doesn't matter how you view The Beatles, there is no denying that John, Paul, George and Ringo are the most recognizable entertainers of the latter half of the twentieth century. Even thirty years after the breakup of the group hardly a day goes past without hearing a mention of the members or a snatch of one of their songs.

At the close of the twentieth century, the media produced numerous polls and retrospectives on nearly all aspects of culture and art. Predominant among them all were The Beatles. But in all the retrospection, one significant moment in the story of The Beatles, and in the development of rock 'n' roll itself, has been overlooked. Or to be more precise, one significant month—January 1956.

In the United States, Elvis Presley's "Heartbreak Hotel" was released to an initially disappointing reaction that had RCA executives wondering if they should have signed Carl Perkins from Sun instead of Elvis. Perkins had just hit the No. 1 spot with "Blue Suede Shoes" while still under contract to Sun Records. What caused RCA's consternation was the fact that they'd paid $35,000 to Sun Records to release Elvis from his contract along with a $50,000 bonus to Elvis himself. But by February "Heartbreak

Hotel" had made it onto the charts and by March 10th had hit the No 1 spot in the US.

By the mid 1950s American rock 'n' roll had also begun to influence the emerging British teenage scene, primarily through the impact of Bill Haley's "Rock Around The Clock" and the early Elvis hits. Suddenly the guitar was the ultimate cool accessory for any teenage boy who wanted to impress the girls, or show off.

The choices facing these teenagers on how to spend their leisure time were also expanding. The local coffee shop soon became a meeting place for teenagers to hang out, exchange ideas, chat and listen to music emanating from the jukebox. In a seaport with close ties to the Trans-Atlantic sea trade like Liverpool, these jukeboxes were often populated with some of the latest American records brought home by merchant seamen.

The British teenage scene had yet to find a voice of its own.

In the same month that "Heartbreak Hotel" was released in the US, an unassuming record by a jazz band banjo player entered the British charts.

"Rock Island Line" by Lonnie Donegan sparked the imagination of thousands of British teenagers desperate for their own sound and musical outlet. For the next two years the British Isles bopped to the sound of numerous amateur "skiffle" bands inspired by Donegan's sound.

What made skiffle music popular was its apparent amateurish nature; you didn't have to read music and the instruments could be fairly basic and homemade. Donegan's innovation was in applying modern production techniques to the basic musical form. That he was able to retain its "playability" makes his achievement all the more noteworthy.

The formal definition of skiffle is "a type of entertainment that mostly black musicians performed at 'rent parties' in the Chicago district of the USA in the 1920s"[1]

The "rent parties" were generally impromptu concerts put together to earn enough to pay the rent. A combination of whoever turned up and what instruments they played, or had made, determined the sound produced. As a result it was difficult to define exactly what type of music was being played. The performers were generally poor, without conventional instruments they sought out any common household object that could be blown, tapped, brushed or converted to make a series of note-like sounds. Common instruments were kettles (with a trumpet mouthpiece attached), washboards (the player wore thimbles on his fingertips and ran them lightly over the corrugated surface to produce the necessary sounds), steel drums (which could either be used as a traditional drum or converted into a bass), or packing crates (which with the addition of a broom handle and string became a bass).

Over a period of time certain homemade instruments began to dominate, a result of their sound and the ease with which they could be obtained. A washboard could easily be used to play a tune in the evening and be back in service for the following day's laundry. The resulting sound became more unified and soon had a name—skiffle*.

Skiffle thrived in the US as a neighborhood movement without ever becoming a commercial hit. As people moved around the country trying to find work, its areas of influence spread. By the late 1940s it was more easily found in the southern states than in the north where it had originated.

It's as a result of this southern migration that skiffle was introduced into Britain. In the early 1950s Jazz was the hottest sound in Britain. Clubs were springing up all over Europe and bands such as The New Paramount Jazz Band and The Crane River Jazz Band were big stars. Looking to extend their repertoire, many bandleaders visited the United States searching for new songs. One popular and obvious destination was New Orleans.

In 1952, Ken Colyer of The Crane River Jazz Band took a trip to the American South returning with several new songs and a new sound, skiffle. Almost immediately on his return to Britain, Colyer began promoting this new sound, not with the Crane River band,

---

*   *The first reference to the name "skiffle" appears to be a 1929 recording "Hometown Skiffle" by American blues singer Charlie Spanel in which all the instruments played are homemade.*

but with his newly formed band aptly named The New Orleans Jazz Band. Among the musicians who joined were trombonist Chris Barber, and banjo player Lonnie Donegan.

The New Orleans Jazz Band only lasted a short time with Chris Barber soon forming his own band which included Donegan and singer/washboard player Beryl Bryden. Both groups began to put skiffle tracks on their albums. And although it was Colyer who was probably skiffle's most active and vocal advocate at the time, it was Barber who had the first commercial success. His first album included skiffle versions of classic American railroad songs such as *John Henry* and *Rock Island Line*. Both tracks featured Lonnie Donegan on lead vocals.

Rock Island Line was released in the UK as a single in January 1956 where it soon entered the Top 10. It was also a #1 hit in the US, reaching the top spot a month before Elvis' *Heartbreak Hotel*. As a result, The Chris Barber Jazz Band went on tour in the States as support for Pat Boone. On the band's return Donegan, fortified by the success of the single, left and formed his own skiffle group. However, Donegan's group had one major difference from those original bands of the 1920s. His lead instrument was now the guitar.

The guitar was on the verge of changing the sound and direction of popular music for generations to come. Donegan's version of skiffle provided the perfect bridge between the music of the past and the music of the future that rebellious teenagers would adopt as their own. The British teenager had at last found a voice.

The impact of Donegan and the skiffle craze can be measured by the rapid increase in guitar sales over this period. From 1950 until 1955 the average number of guitar sales per year in Britain numbered around 5,000; by 1957 it was up to 250,000. It's also estimated that by 1957 there were 5,000 active skiffle groups in Britain.

The skiffle sound was soon commercialized and the BBC even set aside time for youth music programs like Six Five Special and Saturday Skiffle Club (the forerunners of shows like Top Of The Pops and American Bandstand). Despite its popularity and the literally thousands of skiffle groups that appeared between 1956 and 1957, Donegan remained its only real commercial success. In the next 18 months Donegan had a string of ten Top 10 hits, beginning with *Rock Island Line*. But, by the end of 1957, skiffle had peaked in popularity and effectively died away.

Despite its short commercial life, Donegan's brand of skiffle, along with Presley's hip—swiveling antics, would have a lasting impact on teenagers across the British Isles. Among those influenced by Presley's *Heartbreak Hotel* and Donegan's *Rock Island Line* was a diverse group of Liverpool teenagers; 12 year-old George Harrison, 13 year-old James Paul McCartney, 15 year-old Richard Starkey and 15 year-old John Winston Lennon.

Legend has it that John Winston Lennon was born at the height of one of the worst German air-raids on Liverpool, on October 9th 1940 in Oxford Street Maternity Hospital. It is just that, a legend, and one of the many that became attached to John during and after his short life. According to the reports in the Liverpool Echo newspaper archives there were no raids that night or for the next 24 hours. The story probably comes from an oft quoted recollection by his aunt that she had struggled her way across Liverpool during a raid to see the new born John at the hospital. This was probably a few days after his actual birth. But the idea of John being born into a troubled world seemed somehow apt and it became a part of his on-going myth.

John's father, Freddy, was a merchant seaman who had disappeared months earlier and wouldn't re-enter John's life until his son was four when he tried to lure John into emigrating to Australia. A ploy foiled by John's mother Julia.

Julia was a frivolous, pretty, party girl who, after the kidnap attempt, realized that she couldn't give John the steady homelife he needed. She entrusted John to her elder sister, Mimi, and her husband, George, who worked for a small dairy. Over the years Julia took on the role of the fun-loving elder-sister for John with her free spirit and fun-loving nature.

Mimi, on the other hand, was more of a disciplinarian. She was strict, but had a heart of gold, and was determined to give John as good a life as she could. A central part of that philosophy was her aspirations to be seen as firmly middle class, even to the extent of lying about her husband's status at the dairy where he worked and turning a blind eye to his gambling habit. They lived in the quiet Liverpool suburb of Woolton, in the south of the city. In many ways it was the quintessential English middle class suburb of the forties and fifties, almost rural in aspect, with established churches, shops and plenty of open parks, giving the area a leafy aspect despite its relative proximity to the city center.

Mimi also liked to give the impression that she and George were reasonably well off. The truth was that finances were at times stretched and they took in lodgers, primarily students, to help cover expenses at "Mendips". As, in another example of middle-class pretensions, Mimi had named their pre-war semi-detached house at 251 Menlove Avenue, located on a busy main road in Woolton.

Under Mimi's care John soon blossomed and was reading and writing well at age seven, showing early signs of creativity by producing his own illustrated books. He also developed a keen sense of the absurd from listening to The Goon Show on the radio, a precursor to the anarchic style of humor later popularized by Monty Python, as well as immersing himself in Alice in Wonderland amongst other books.

John's first school was Dovedale Primary School, where the headmaster was so impressed with him he told Mimi that John was "*as sharp as a needle.*[2]" His religious needs were addressed by attendance at St. Peter's Sunday School with his best friend Peter Shotton.

Although it sounds like an idyllic early childhood, John recalled that under the façade he was already living another life. One of manipulation and sometimes physical violence—where John was not the victim but the perpetrator. "*Other boy's parents hated me, They were always warning their kids not to play with me.*[3]"

At the age of 11 John passed the required state examinations and was accepted to Quarry Bank High School alongside his mate, Pete Shotton.

Pete Shotton was a tall boy, slim, with blond hair who lived just around the corner from John at 83 Vale Road. Also living on Vale Road were two other members of the St Peter's Sunday School crowd and members of "John's Gang," Ivan Vaughan and Nigel Walley. They would both have roles to play in upcoming months. In Ivan's case it would be a very pivotal role that would facilitate one of the most significant moments in rock history.

On arrival at Quarry Bank, John continued his aggressive ways in an effort to establish himself as a leader. In a desperate attempt to become popular, he and Pete Shotton soon established themselves as the "class clowns" always good for a joke and a lark. As they worked their way up the school their grades fell.

When John was thirteen his Uncle George died and left a void in John's life. While Mimi was the figure of discipline and rules in the house, Uncle George had been the quiet rebel, giving John far more leeway. Into this void stepped his mother, Julia, and John would rush back to her whenever he had any sort of confrontation with Mimi.

By 1956 John was in the bottom class and ranked 20th out of 20 pupils, Academically he couldn't fall any lower. Music would be his salvation.

Although John Lennon appeared to have little money of his own to spend, he parted with some of his cash to buy a fragile 10 inch 78 rpm record of Lonnie Donegan's *Rock Island Line*. The large solid vinyl single was played over and over again. When it was well worn the enterprising John sold it to his school friend, Rod Davis for half-a-crown (two shillings and six pence). Davis is still in possession of this unique piece of memorabilia.[4]

Rod Davis was pretty much the opposite of John Lennon and Pete Shotton and the fact that they were ever really friends is still surprising. At Quarry Bank, Rod was one of the "swots," keen to do the right thing, be a conformist, an excellent student. But living at 129 Kings Drive in Woolton, he had also been a regular at the St. Peter's Sunday School and was therefore a familiar face for John when they all arrived at the large high school. As an old fashioned traditional school, Quarry Bank still employed the house system. Rod ended up in Woolton House, alongside Pete Shotton, Eric Griffiths and John Lennon.

While John found something in Donegan's musical style that would provide an outlet, it was Elvis that inspired him to play. From the moment he first heard *Heartbreak Hotel*, the young John Lennon couldn't get enough of Elvis.

> *"To me rock n roll was real, everything else was unreal. It was the only thing to get through to me, of all the things that were happening to me when I was 15."*[5]

The direct result was that John was soon pestering his dispersed family for a guitar. The first to succumb to this pressure was, unsurprisingly, his mother Julia. John had spotted an advert for a secondhand "Spanish Guitar—guaranteed not to break" in the back of the popular Reveille Magazine. The musically inclined Julia scraped together the necessary £10 and soon John was the proud owner of a ¾ sized Gallotone Champion flat top acoustic guitar. This guitar was auctioned at Sothebys in September 1999 along with a collection of John's 78rpm records, which included "*Lost John/Stewball*" and "*Cumberland Gap/Love is Strange*", both by Donegan. There was also an unused guitar tutor book and photo of Lonnie torn from a newspaper.

There is some argument as to whether John had played an instrument earlier in his childhood and so already had a basic understanding of musical form. In fact friend Rod Davis recalls that this guitar was in fact John's second, and that he had earlier been in possession of a Egmond guitar, but it's origin remains something of a mystery[6]. John himself recalled that initially he used to borrow a guitar. "*I couldn't play, but a pal of mine had one and it fascinated me.*"[7] At least one source[8] suggests that John had tried to learn, and abandoned, the accordion as a child and had been given a harmonica by one of the students who lodged at "Mendips." Other sources[9] suggest he was given a harmonica by his Uncle George and that on a lengthy bus trip to stay with relatives in Edinburgh, Scotland one summer he had been taught to play it by the bus driver. Others argue that John's ability to push the musical boundaries later in life was as a direct result of his "ignorance" and lack of formal music training.

Whichever view you subscribe to, it's well accepted that this cheap mail-order guitar was John's first real exposure to the instrument that would allow him to lead a whole new generation of popular artists. Julia Lennon, a fairly good banjo player, set about teaching her son how to play the guitar by tuning the top four strings to G (just like a banjo), the bottom two strings being tuned the same as the fourth[10]. Having set-up his guitar in this style, Julia showed him a few basic banjo style chords. Armed with this basic knowledge John applied himself to learning his first real tune—Fats Dominio's *"Ain't That A Shame.*[11]*"*

While Julia was an active supporter of John's new interest, his Aunt Mimi wasn't—seeing it as just another of John's obsessional "phases." His constant twanging on the guitar became intolerable for Mimi and she banished John to the enclosed front porch at "Mendips." It didn't take long before the repeated hammering of banjo chords started to take a toll on the cheap guitar and John began to pester Mimi to buy him a newer, better guitar. Hearing the strange sounds emanating from this instrument John's Aunt Mimi relented and bought him a guitar from Hessy's music shop in Whitechapel. Hessy's Music Store was located in close proximity to the future locations of both The Cavern and Brian Epstein's NEMS music store. Over the years most of the Liverpool bands bought their instrument there—usually on very favorable credit terms. Shop manager Jim Gretty sold Mimi a Spanish model with steel strings for around £17.

While Elvis was at the forefront of John's mind, it wasn't long before he discovered that there were other great R&B singers out there as well. John's introduction to the pantheon of American R&B singers came via a school friend, Mike Hill.

> *"This boy at school had been to Holland. He said he'd got this record at home by somebody who was better than Elvis... The new record was 'Long Tall Sally'. When I heard it, it was so great I couldn't speak."*[12]

John had discovered Little Richard and was soon on a mission to hear and find out as much about American R&B music and the roots of rock 'n' roll as he could. John's almost encyclopedic knowledge of rock 'n' roll on both sides of the Atlantic, and his ability to draw on it, was one of the things that ultimately set The Beatles apart from the other emerging Liverpool bands of the period.

February 1956

On the 24th of February George Harrison officially became a teenager as he celebrated his 13th Birthday. George was born at 12 Arnold Grove, Wavertree Liverpool on 24th February 1943. He was the youngest of three children born to Harry and Louise Harrison. While George's surroundings and upbringing were distinctly working class, his father was a bus driver, they were comfortable and probably the most supportive and "normal" of all the Beatles.

When George was six the family moved to a house at 25 Upton Green in Speke, George attended the local Dovedale primary at the same time that John was there, although several years behind. The two never meet. While not an outstanding student he did well enough to pass the entrance requirements for the prestigious Liverpool Institute and started at the city center school in 1954. Riding to the school on his father's Number 86 bus between Speke Boulevard and Mount Street, a journey of just under an hour, he soon made the acquaintance of another Liverpool Institute pupil and Speke resident, one James Paul McCartney.

Liverpool Institute was old enough for Dickens to have performed public readings there. It's once grand building was fading behind its imposing Greek façade and was generally in poor repair and stocked with outdated school fittings. It was not unusual to find desks marked with initials scratched into the surface more than forty years previously.

After the war the school building had been portioned to provide homes for a dance and drama academy and the fledgling Liverpool Art College.

George was not a particularly memorable pupil in his early

years being quiet and somewhat introverted. But the passive behavior soon transformed into signs of rebellion as homework started to be completed on the bus journey home, or he would get the parents approval signature on his report card forged by the obliging mother of a friend so his own parents wouldn't find out that his grades were slipping.

Within the space of a couple of terms George and his friends, Arthur Kelley and Tony Workman, were known as truants, a good source of smutty stories and the leaders of the kids who had swapped playground candy for a smoke behind the bike sheds. The gang of truants would spend their afternoons at the Jacey Cinema in Clayton Square, feeding George's interest in movies.

At the age of 12 George was attracted by a poster to visit the 1955 British Grand Prix motor race that was being held that year at Liverpool's Aintree circuit. He made the journey by bus and train to watch the event and was captivated by the sights and sounds of motor racing. It would remain a life long passion. George took to motor racing like most other Liverpool boys took to soccer. But instead of the stars of the two local soccer teams on his bedroom walls, George had pictures of race cars, many taken with his faithful box camera.

And of course there was music, and Elvis in particular. Thanks to Arthur Kelley's sister, Barbara, whose fiancée was a ship's engineer, George had access to a steady supply of American rock 'n' roll records long before they were released to the UK market (if ever). In fact, most teenagers in Liverpool knew someone who had some connection to one of the many shipping companies that traded through the busy dock area.

As the skiffle craze spread through Liverpool, George discussed forming a band with his brother Pete, who already owned a battered guitar well past its prime, and Arthur Kelley. Arthur's kind hearted grandmother made the first investment in George's musical ambitions by buying him a three-penny washboard from a local market. But the idea of forming a group never got beyond the talking stage.

As he became a teenager, George's parents noticed this new

interest was starting to take hold of George. He was expressing it in a passion for guitars. He was bringing home school note books covered with drawings of guitars, of all shapes and sizes. That interest lead to its inevitable conclusion when George arrived home with the news that a boy at school had a guitar for sale for three pounds, would his parents buy it for him?

> *"When I was 13 or 14, I was sat at the back of class trying to draw guitars in school note books. I was totally into guitars. I heard about this kid at school who had a guitar for (sale at) £3/10, it was just a little acoustic round hole. I got the £3/10 from my mother—that was a lot of money for us, then."*[13]

As George recalls, his parents managed to find the cash and George was soon the proud owner of a beat up Dutch Egmond flat top acoustic guitar that was held together by a single screw attaching the neck to the body. Before strumming a single note he started striking poses in front of the mirror in imitation of Elvis. To George the guitar felt natural, as if it belonged in his hands.

It didn't take long for the posing to be replaced by the first halting steps at trying to produce a tune; unfortunately George's admittedly clumsy first steps were too much for the precarious hold of the screw, which was soon dislodged. Frustrated and unable to reattach the neck, George put the guitar in a cupboard and promptly forgot about it.

May 1956

After a gap of almost three months, George retrieved his broken guitar from the cupboard where it had been discarded. He handed it over to his older brother Pete in the hope that he could succeed in reattaching the neck. Luckily Pete Harrison's skills with a screwdriver and patience exceeded those of his younger sibling and effective repairs were soon made. George now began to practice in earnest.

George had begun to show an aversion to formal teaching that was impacting his schooling. But he was determined to teach himself to master the guitar. Armed with a series of guitar manuals including Bert Weedon's *Play In A Day* book, George soon realized that he wasn't a natural musician. But with encouragement from the family, and his mother, Louise, in particular, he would practice at every available opportunity. Often playing so long that his fingers would start to bleed.

George's devotion to his new passion spurred his brother Pete to dig his own old guitar out of storage and join in the practice sessions. Soon the pair could be found picking out the tunes from favorite songs heard on the radio or the few records they had access to.

> *"Whatever (rock-n-roll record) was playing on the radio we'd try and listen to it. You couldn't even get a cup of sugar•, never mind a rock n roll record."*[14]
>
> *"I'd study the way the words were written and sung,"* George later recalled, *"then I'd go over them myself. I bought a little book with all the chords. I couldn't make head nor tail of it, but I forced my fingers to put out the right chords."*[15]

June 1956

Across the golf course from "Mendips" and John Lennon, another music mad teenager celebrated his 14th Birthday on the 18th, a certain James Paul McCartney.

Young James was born on 18th June 1942 and in keeping with family tradition was given the same first name as his father, great grandfather and great-great grandfather. To avoid family confusion the eldest McCartney son was referred to by his middle name, Paul.

His father Jim had at one time held musical ambitions, playing piano and trumpet. He even led his own band "Jim Mac's Jazz

---

• *Rationing of food, introduced during World War Two, had only recently (1954) been abolished in the UK*

Band" playing many of the same dance halls around Liverpool that his son was destined to frequent. However, his dream of a life in show business never really materialized and he drifted into the cotton industry to provide a steady living wage. At the outbreak of war he started working at the Napier engineering works as a lathe turner and helped fight the fires left from German bombing raids as a volunteer fireman. Paul's mother had been a nursing sister in charge of the maternity wing where Paul, and eighteen months later, his brother Micheal, were born. She left the hospital to raise her young family and worked as a district health visitor assisting local families left destitute by the bombing.

After the war Jim returned to his previous job as a cotton salesman while Paul's mother, Mary, became a domiciliary midwife. But the cotton industry was in rapid decline and Jim's earnings suffered. Times were hard for the McCartney family and they often moved as the demands on Mary's time and the location of her "rounds" changed. Eventually they ended up in the area of Liverpool known as Speke.

Speke is located on the fields of ancient pig farms that once surrounded the city of Liverpool. It took its name for the Anglo-Saxon "Spic" meaning bacon. In 1936 the hamlet of Speke was chosen as the location for a new "model town" of 35,000 houses. Despite being planned with parks, playing fields and enough schools to go around it was a fairly soulless place.

For the McCartney boys, school was the nearby Stockton Wood Road primary school. As Speke continued to expand, the school was soon overcrowded and even held the dubious honor of being the largest junior school in Britain with 1500 pupils on its books. The solution to the overcrowding was to bus a select number of students, including the McCartney boys, over half an hour away to Joseph Williams Primary School in Belle Vale, Gateacre—another purpose built suburb.

In the early fifties the McCartney family moved once again, this time to 12 Ardwick Road in Speke on the expanding Eastern edge of the estate. The road and the surrounding fields were a permanent building site.

In 1953 Paul was one of only 4 pupils from the Joseph Williams School to score high enough points in the state mandated eleven-plus examination to gain entrance into the prestigious Liverpool Institute, the city's top grammar school.

The daily commute to the city center was soon enlivened by the presence of a young neighbor, George Harrison. The two soon fell into conversation and once they discovered a common interest in music and guitars, and developed a fast friendship, despite being in different years at school. Although one year ahead at school, Paul tended to look down on his younger friend and sometimes be a little patronizing. Within a few years, George would prove to be a more talented with the guitar than Paul.

Paul recalled "*We lived a bus stop apart. I'd get on the bus to school and at the next stop George would get on. We were close in age and had the same interests so it was natural for us to sit next to each other. He was about 18 months younger, which is a big difference at that age. I guess it's a failing of mine that I always tended to talk down to him as I'd known him as a young kid*"[16].

The bus ride became a place to swap stories and ideas. Paul McCartney has always claimed that this daily bus ride served as the inspiration for the start of "A Day In The Life" (Beatles—Sgt. Peppers' Lonely Hearts Club Band). As his morning routine was to "*get* (sleepily) *out of bed/dragged a comb across his head/caught the bus/ went upstairs* (to meet George) / *had a smok*e—(usually an untiped Woodbine) / *went into a* (day)*dream./*)

George recalls that Paul and he were already getting together for the occasional jam session even at this early stage in their friendship. "*Paul and I used to get together and play a bit. Just school boys. There was no groups involved until later*[17]."

1955 saw a change in Mary's job that meant the McCartney family moved for one last time to number 20 Forthlin Road in the nearby suburb of Allerton. Although not far from Speke, Allerton (literally "the place of the alders") was a world apart in attitude and pretensions. Astutely class conscious the residents of Allerton strove to be firmly middle class, and Mary McCartney soon was affecting her speech and trying to "better" herself, in an almost identical way to John Lennon's Aunt Mimi living across the golf course in nearby Woolton.

Despite their father's background as a musician and band leader, neither of the McCartney boys showed much inclination towards a career in music as children. Their father did arrange piano lessons for them, but made the mistake of scheduling the lessons during the summer vacation when young Paul and Mike McCartney would have rather been outside running around with their mates. So the kind hearted Jim McCartney let them quit on the condition that Paul tried out for a spot in the Liverpool Cathedral Choir. The story is that Paul deliberately cracked his voice during the audition, although prophetically enough, he did spend a short time as a chorister at the church of St. Chad's located just off a certain Penny Lane.

Around late 1954 or early 1955 Paul inherited an old trumpet from his father and learnt to pick out a few tunes such as "When The Saints Go Marching In." However, he preferred singing and realized that a trumpet was not exactly conducive to being able to sing• and "traded it in" for a guitar of uncertain heritage, a Zenith Model 17 acoustic with ∫-holes, which at first he couldn't figure out. As Paul recalls "*it wasn't until I found a picture of Slim Whitman, who was also left handed, and saw that I had the guitar the wrong way round.*[18]" Paul had the instrument re-strung so he could play it "upside down."

July 1956

On the 7th of July, across town in the area of Liverpool that's known as "The Dingle" a young Richard Starkey celebrated his 16th Birthday. Young Richard was born a week late in 1940 and first saw the light of day in the front bedroom of his parents house at 9 Madryn Street. The Starkey family had been residents of the Dingle for well over a century, but young "Richie" always seem to strive for better things in life and often expressed a desire to grow

---

• *The other reason suggested for Paul's abandonment of the trumpet is that it gave him blisters on his lips which didn't look attractive and would "put off any girls"*

up and have "*a semi in a posh part of Liverpool.*[19]" like his cousins who lived in more affluent Crosby.

For reasons that he never fully understood, Richie's parents divorced when he was just three years old and he was left to be raised single handedly by his mother Elsie. A year after the divorce the Starkey's moved to 10 Admiral Grove where the rent was cheaper. Plus it had the advantage of being close to Elsie's place of work, the Empress Pub.

Located a short five minute walk away from their new house, St. Silas Infants School was to be Richie's first experience of education, for a short time at least. For at age six he was rushed to hospital with what at first was diagnosed as a burst appendix, but soon progressed to peritonitis. Little Richie slipped into a coma for nearly two months. The road to recovery was long and his only distraction was the "ward band" where Richie was always the first to volunteer to hit the tin drum.

Richie returned to school where he was placed in a class with kids a year younger, but his progress was still slow. Even private tutoring didn't help his unorthodox spelling and he wasn't allowed to take the Eleven plus examination for the local Grammar School. Instead he was placed at Dingle Vale Secondary Modern—the place where the "failures" were sent.

To escape his difficult educational experience and continuing illnesses, Richie became a devotee of the cinema and the Westerns in particular. His first musical hero was Gene Autry, and he rapidly developed a liking for American style Country & Western music, which, like rock 'n' roll, was more prevalent in Liverpool than in other British cities due to the influx of transatlantic seamen.

However by 1952 Richie's absences from school, 34 occasions in one term alone, were no longer purely due to his health. Truancy was often to blame as Richie discovered cigarettes and alcohol. The matinee cowboys were replaced by science fiction movies and role models like James Dean.

Things improved for Richie when his mother married, with Richie's permission, Harry Graves, a painter and decorator from Romford in Essex. Unfortunately a trip to meet Harry's family in the south of England resulted in another hospital stay. A soaking during a thunderstorm had quickly developed into chronic pleurisy. Moved from hospital to hospital, Richie eventually spent a considerable time at the Heswell Children's Hospital on the Wirral peninsula across the River Mersey from his home town. Deemed well enough to go home by 1955, his schooling was now officially over and employment beckoned.

His first job offer would be as a deliver boy for British Rail, provided he agreed to a brief secondment at Riversdale Technical College to complete his education. He agreed to the educational requirements, attended a few classes and then failed the medical.

Next try was as a barman-waiter on the ferry across the Mersey (later immortalized in song by Gerry & The Pacemakers). Richie worked hard, and played hard too—especially at the weekends, the parties helped along by Richie's ready access to the miniature bottles of liquor served on the ferry. Unfortunately after one such weekend party, still fuelled with "Dutch courage" he told his supervisor the truth about where his supply of drinks came from, and was promptly sacked.

Richie's step-father managed to persuade the owners of a nearby Engineering company, Henry Hunt & Sons, manufactures of gymnasium and swimming pool equipment, to take on his stepson as an apprentice joiner.

By 1956 the 16 year old Richie Starkey was a working apprentice with a liking for the good things in life, and a seemingly natural talent for tapping out the rhythm for almost any song he heard. He had also taught himself a basic "three chord trick" on the guitar and a similar one on the piano. But lacked the interest or the application to take these early musical experiments any further.

September 1956

September meant a return to school after the long summer break, a time to renew friendships. The bus ride to the Liverpool Institute was the perfect opportunity for George and Paul to discuss their growing mutual interest in rock 'n' roll and guitars.

The return to school this year would also be of particular significance to John and the foundation of what would eventually evolve into The Beatles. Perhaps the most controversial date amongst Beatles historians is the exact date of the founding of John Lennon's first group—The Quarry Men[♦]. John himself placed the date as being 1955[20], while several works place it at March 1957[21]. However surviving Quarry Men, Eric Griffiths, Pete Shotton, Rod Davis, Colin Hanton and Len Garry put the date as the period between September and October 1956. Len Garry's 1997 book provides the first real documented testimonial to the start of The Quarry Men from participants other than John Lennon, whose recall of early events and dates was notoriously suspect. Rod Davis also confirmed that *"Our latest thinking puts the start of the group in late 1956.*[22]*"*

According to Eric Griffiths[23] the idea of forming a band was suggested to John by a mutual friend called George Lee. All three were students at Quarry Bank School, not far from their homes. Quarry Bank was a traditional British grammar school of the period whose sole responsibility was to turn provincial boys into candidates for University. It was still run on traditional lines complete with a Latin motto "Hoc ex metallo virtutem" (Out of this quarry cometh forth manhood) and a school song that all new boys had to learn.

Apparently George Lee had noticed John's increasing fascination with the guitar and early in the new school year, September 1956, suggested to John that he might form a skiffle band of his own. John wasn't immediately struck by the idea. After all John saw himself as a creative, unique individual; not a follower of fashion. But he began to mull over the idea and a few weeks later announced to Pete Shotton that he was thinking of starting a skiffle group. While he saw himself as a leader, John needed the support of those he felt closest too, forming a group with a bunch of strangers with similar interests would never have occurred to him, instead he reached out to his friends.

♦ *The name of John's skiffle group has been written as one or two words in a variety of publications. In the school song from which it was taken it appears as one word, but on the photographs of the group it is clearly spelt as two words on the drum face, for this reason I have decided to stick with "Quarry Men."*

> "It'll be a laugh—even if it doesn't come to anything. Let's give it a try."[24]

John was OK as he had his guitar and knew a few basic chords, but Pete needed an instrument to play. In the best skiffle tradition they scrounged up a couple of instruments by raiding the storeroom of Pete's mother's wool shop. The search yielded a washboard and a disused tea chest. With a discarded broom handle and a piece of string the chest was soon converted into a typical skiffle bass. They now had three instruments, but only two players.

John and Pete's search for an additional player for their nescient group returned to their only available source of talent, Quarry Bank. Asking around among their friends at school failed to solicit any volunteers, so John posted a notice asking for anyone interested in playing bass in a new skiffle group. He received only one reply, from a kid named Bill Smith who was instantly recruited.

The trio once more made good use of the kindness of Peter Shotton's family by practicing in an old air-raid shelter at the bottom of the Shotton garden. In the immediate post-war years air-raid shelters were still common with large communal ones built at the end of streets while some houses had smaller ones built in the back gardens. Many of these lasted into the sixties and seventies being converted into storage sheds, aquariums, potting sheds etc. In fact the post war years in the UK was still a period of depravation with government imposed austerity measures and food rationing a way of life. It's not surprising that teenagers growing up in this environment were attracted to the rebelliousness of rock 'n' roll and the promises of a better life it seemed to exude.

October 1956

By early October, around the time of his 16th Birthday on the 9th, John was on the look out for more talent to join his group. He made tracks to pull in Eric Griffiths, the only other guitar player at school, who lived about 15 minutes away from John in Halewood Drive on the other side of Woolton Village.

Eric, proud owner of a Dutch Egmond acoustic, wasn't part of the St. Peter's Sunday School crowd, only having arrived in Woolton from Wales the year before starting at Quarry Bank. However the first day at Quarry Bank he found himself in form 1R along side John Lennon and Pete Shotton. Although a serious boy by nature, he and John bonded due to shared circumstances. Eric lost his father, a pilot, during the war.

Another, albeit indirect, target of John's overtures was his classmate Rod Davis. Rod was closer to Eric Griffiths than he was to John and told Eric that he had purchased a banjo the day before. Rod's uncle had told him about a man in North Wales he knew who was selling a guitar. By the time Rod got there, the guitar had been sold, but the man had a Windsor White Victor Supremo banjo for sale. Rod bought the banjo and Eric immediately invited him to join the fledgling group[25].

Knowing that Rod had only just acquired his instrument, John and Eric set about teaching him their basic system of playing. This was to play everything in a single key, C, and employ only three chords, C, F, G7. Early rehearsals were punctuated by Eric Griffiths shouting the chord changes to Rod as John sang.

Rehearsals now alternated between the Shotton's air-raid shelter and Eric Griffiths' home. During one such rehearsal, Eric mentioned that he had a friend who owned a set of drums. John immediately ordered Eric to go off and find his friend Colin who he had meet on a bus ride a few months earlier.

Colin was different from John's other recruits in that he was older and had already left school the year before. He was two years older than John and lived on the other side of Woolton at 4 Heyscroft Road. But none of that mattered. He had a drum set, and as time was to prove over and over again, finding a drummer was not the easiest thing in the world. Colin's precious £38 drum kit had been purchased from Hessy's with a portion of his wages as an apprentice upholsterer at a local furniture factory. Colin recalls that his "call to arms" happened one Sunday in the late summer of 1956 when there was a knock on his front door. It was Eric inviting him to a rehearsal at his house. Colin packed up his John Gray

Broadway drum kit, comprising of a small bass drum, floor tom, tom-tom, snare drum and cymbal, and took it around to the house where he "auditioned" for John, Pete and a couple of other people (he can't recall who). "*I played a bit on my drums—and that was it. I was invited to join the group, there and then.*"[26] By the end of the rehearsal, Colin Hanton, and his prized Broadway drum kit, had joined the still unnamed band. Colin also supplied another practice venue as his house soon became the regular Saturday afternoon meeting place.

The group struggled to come up with a name that they all could identify with and after a few suggestions, agreed on the name "The Blackjacks." It's been suggested that this name may have come from the fact that most of the group tended to wear a combination of black jeans and white shirts[27]—fairly common garb for young rockers of the period. They obviously didn't identify with the name that strongly as within a week it had been changed to "The Quarry Men," inspired by both the name of the school which the majority of group members attended and the line from the school song "*Quarrymen old before our birth.*"[28]

Around the same time that the group decided on a name, it also went through its first major change in line-up. During mid to late October Bill Smith had given up coming to rehearsals. When he failed to show, John's friends Ivan Vaughan or Nigel Walley would take his place. But, the group needed a permanent reliable replacement. In late October 1956 Len Garry was asked to join.

Len was the first member of The Quarry Men not to be a pupil at Quarry Bank, or live in Woolton. Len lived at 77 Lance Lane in Wavertree, another middle-class suburb of Liverpool. He attended Mosspits Primary School where Pete Shotton was the year ahead of him, although neither recalls knowing each other at that point[29]. Len proved to be a good student and passed the entrance qualifications for the prestigious Liverpool Institute where he became good friends with Ivan Vaughan. It was through this connection that he was drawn into John Lennon's sphere of influence, meeting him during the 1955 summer vacation period, and being invited to join The Quarry Men. Len didn't really want to play the tea-chest bass, he wanted to be the singer. But John was firm about being the singer himself, so Len settled for the bass.

Unaware that his services were no longer required Bill Smith took the tea-chest bass home with him after eventually turning up for a rehearsal. John and Pete Shotton ducked out of school for an afternoon to "steal it back" so it could be passed on to Len. And in a pattern that was to be repeated several times during the early development of The Beatles[*], John couldn't bring himself to face the unfortunate Smith and asked another, in this case Pete Shotton, to pass on the news of his dismissal.

The songs rehearsed by the early Quarry Men were largely based on standard skiffle hits employed by any number of the thousands of amateur skiffle bands that were popping up all over Britain. Hits such as ROCK ISLAND LINE, JOHN HENRY, DON'T YOU ROCK ME DADDYO, FREIGHT TRAIN and WORRIED MAN BLUES.

The addition of this later song to the Quarry Men's repertoire was the catalyst for bringing to the fore John Lennon's unique skills at word play. Most of the songs were transcribed by listening to records or copying from the radio. In the case of this particular Burl Ives song the 78rpm record that the group was using as source material was well worn and scratched and, as a result John had a hard time hearing the lyrics. Most people would have given up and dropped the song from their play list, but not The Quarry Men and not John Lennon. John felt that it was the sound, not the words that were important. So he set about replacing the words he couldn't make out with a few improvisations of his own. On occasions he would even re-title the song, as he did when he transformed "Streamlined Train" into the Quarry Men number LONG BLACK TRAIN[30].

---

[*] *Perhaps most infamously with the dismissal of drummer Pete Best in 1962 on the verge of their recording career.*

Rod Davis recalls that *"What we did was to listen to the latest singles when they were played on the radio and try to copy the words down. The trouble was if you couldn't make them out or write them down quickly enough you were stuck. So what John used to do was to add his own words. No-one ever seemed to notice because they didn't know the words either."*[31]

While the month of October marked the birth of The Quarry Men, it also brought death into the life of a future member. For on October 31st Mary McCartney, Paul's beloved mother, died suddenly of breast cancer.

Desperate to protect her two sons, she had kept the illness secret until it was too late to do anything about it. She eventually was admitted into hospital just two days before her death.

The impact on Paul and his family was immense, not only from an emotional but from a financial point of view. There is an often repeated story that Paul's reaction to the news of his mother's passing was *"What are we going to do without her money?"* But perhaps more indicative of Paul's' true reaction is that he now immersed himself in his music, letting his emotions play out in his songwriting, including his first song I LOST MY LITTLE GIRL. According to Paul's brother Mike, the elder McCartney *"Lost a mother but found the guitar."*[32]

November 1956

As The Quarry Men were settling on a line-up and putting together their initial song list, the man responsible for their existence came to town. On Monday 5th[33] November 1956 Lonnie Donegan played The Liverpool Empire[34].

Unable to get tickets for the event, Paul McCartney stood outside in the crowds around the stage door just to get a glimpse of his idol. From that moment on Paul clamored for a new guitar to replace the old Zenith. Despite their financial difficulties, his father Jim relented and traded it up for a £15 Rosati "Lucky Seven" which initially only had two strings. Despite this handicap Paul and his guitar were now inseparable, he took it everywhere including the bathroom.

Along with the renewed passion for the guitar game a growing awareness of rock 'n' roll music that soon replaced Paul's preference for old show tunes, although he never lost that early love of a "nice tune."

Before long Paul was joined by classmate Ian James in cycling around Liverpool dressed in "teddy boy" style narrow drainpipe trousers, with guitars strapped to their backs searching out places to play.

One person who did mange to attend the Donegan concert was a young George Harrison. In fact George borrowed money from his parents and attended every show, accompanied by his brother's girlfriend. Young George was so enamoured of Donegan and his music that when he found out that Lonnie Donegan was staying near his house in Speke, he went around and hammered on the door until he got the skiffle star's autograph.

PART TWO

"Lennon & McCartney"—1957

January 1957

As the Quarry Men refined their line up and struggled to learn new songs, a new venue opened in central Liverpool as a showcase for more accomplished local musicians. On the 16th January 1957 The Merseyside Jazz Union officially opened drawing substantial crowds. It wasn't long before this latest hangout became better known by its unofficial name—The Cavern.

The Cavern was owned and operated by Alan Sytner, the son of a local doctor, and an old school friend of one Brian Epstein. Sytner, like many young men of the time, was a jazz enthusiast. He organized the occasional jazz night at the Temple restaurant in Liverpool but wanted to find a location with more ambience suited to the sounds and mood of the jazz crowd. Jazz filled the gap between the war-time big band sound and the emergence of rock 'n' roll. By the late 1950s jazz was the favorite musical genre for people in their early twenties, especially those of a more "artistic" inclination. In common with many other jazz enthusiasts from prosperous families, Alan Sytner made a pilgrimage to Paris, the epicenter of European jazz innovation at the time. There, in 1956, he became enamoured with one particular club, "La Caveau." Sytner became convinced that a similar city-center, cellar type club would be a success in his native Liverpool and on his return began to search for a suitable location.

He found it in Mathew Street. Or to be strictly accurate, underneath Mathew Street in central Liverpool. The area had been the original "fruit packing" area of Liverpool given its proximity to both the docks and the city center. Mathew Street at the time was a dark, dingy, little-used thoroughfare with seven story warehouses on either side and, as a consequence, little natural sunlight penetrated as far as the narrow sidewalk. Many warehouses had vacant cellars that had been used at one time or another for activities such as storing wine or egg-packing. During the war most had been used as air-raid shelters and now lay in disuse. Warehouse owners were offering rental on them for as cheap as 10 shillings a week.

Alan Sytner rented the cellar spaces underneath numbers 8, 9 and 10 Mathew Street and began the task of converting them into a jazz club. Entrance was to be through a "hole in the wall" at number 10. The descent was down a short flight of 18 winding stone steps that "*gave about enough room for one person to go down, you couldn't pass anyone on the stairs it was that narrow. The stairs went to nothing on one side so you had to go down sideways. You got to the bottom and you were in a basement, a very smelly dingy place that was always damp.*[35]." At the bottom was a table which acted as an admissions booth.

The Cavern's interior is familiar to many fans from the numerous photographs taken during The Beatles' later residence. It consisted of three long arches with the small stage located at the far end of the center arch. "*The stage was built into an arch and the groups didn't have a terrific amount of headroom. If you look at the photographs, the two* (group members stood) *nearest the wall are always bent over because the arch would touch the top of their heads. They probably had about six feet of usable playing space out of the 14 foot stage.*[36]" Initially seating was also supplied in the center arch with dancing restricted to the outer archways.

The Club was also alcohol free with only soda being served from its small bar. Alan Sytner's original plan was to have Traditional Jazz on Saturday, Modern Jazz on Thursday with Skiffle relegated to Wednesday nights.

Opening night was headlined by resident house band "The Merseysippi Jazz Band." It's estimated that around 1000 people lined up in Mathew Street on that opening night waiting to crush into the club, which had a nominal capacity of 600. That was a foretaste of what was to come.

February 1957

Over in the area of Liverpool known as "The Dingle," on the edge of the river between the city center and Garston, several miles away from Woolton, the skiffle craze was just as popular, although its proponents tended more towards the country and western sound than rock 'n' roll.

Repeating a scenario that was familiar all over the city, two friends decided to get together and form a group as a distraction from their run of the mill day jobs. It was a chance to have a few laughs and maybe earn some beer money. Eddie Mills had a guitar and his next door neighbor, Richard Starkey, had been hammering away on a cheap drum kit during lunch break at work. Eddie came up with a stage name of "Eddie Clayton*" and invited his friend, neighbor and work-mate, to join him to provide the rhythm section of The Eddie Clayton Skiffle Group.

Other members were recruited from their place of work, Hunt & Sons, a local engineering company that manufactured school playground equipment. The line up was Eddie "Clayton" Miles on guitar, Richard Starkey on drums, Roy Trafford on tea-chest bass, Johnny Dougherty on washboard and the only non-Hunts employee, Frank Walsh on guitar.

Richie's drum set had been procured for him by his step father Harry during a trip to Romford and dutifully transported all the way back to Liverpool on the train. Richie was delighted with the second hand set, a Broadway "Kat" snare and symbol outfit that normally sold for £10

The newest arrival on the Liverpool skiffle scene started out playing a few lunch time sessions at the works canteen before securing their

---

* *Years later Ringo would suggest that Eric Clapton use the name "Eddie Clayton" as a pseudonym for the work he did on "The Beatles" (aka The White Album).*

first gig at the Labour Club in Peel Street, Toxteth. From there, they took the familiar route of talent shows where they failed miserably.

March 1957

The Quarry Men's rehearsals were continuing apace but no bookings were forthcoming. Although they were starting to play at friends parties, none of them were particularly good musicians. However they were already beginning to notice that John could "hold an audience.[37]" John's friend Nigel Walley, who had attended most of the practice sessions, even picking up the washboard on occasions, showed his entrepreneurial spirit by offering to "manage" The Quarry Men.

Nigel quickly came to the conclusion that the group* would never get a paying gig if no-one knew they existed. Playing in each others front rooms wasn't the way to get noticed, so he had a series of business cards printed that were posted in local shop windows.

> "COUNTRY, WESTERN, ROCK 'N' ROLL, SKIFFLE
> THE QUARRY MEN
> OPEN FOR ENGAGEMENTS"

The inclusion of "Country" and "Western" reflects the musical inclination of both Nigel and Quarry Men banjo player Rod Davis. But, there's no record of The Quarry Men ever learning or playing any country & western style numbers. Skiffle was still the predominant style of song they performed with the number of rock 'n' roll songs in their repertoire was rapidly growing.

April 1957

Rehearsals at Eric Griffith's house were becoming more difficult and the group was looking around for places to rehearse.

---

*   *Len Garry wrote that The Quarry Men always referred to themselves as "the group" even from the earliest days, and never as a "band."*

John's interest in music and playing the guitar had brought him closer to his mother than he'd been for a long time. When she heard of the search for a new place to practice John's mother Julia offered the use of the house she shared with her common-law "husband" John Dykins .The Quarry Men soon relocated their rehearsals to the bathroom at Blomfield Road in Allerton where to their delight they found that the acoustics were superior. They must have made a strange sight with various group members stood in the bathtub or perched precariously on the edge of the sink and toilet as they played. Julia Lennon also occasionally joined her son and his friends, adding her banjo playing to the already eclectic sound that The Quarry Men produced.

Around the same time, Pete Shotton's mother learnt from an overheard conversation with a local shopkeeper that there were plans for a garden fete at St. Peters Church in nearby Woolton sometime in July. Pete, along his friend John Lennon, had attended Sunday School at the church when younger, so Mrs. Shotton knew the vicar, The Reverend Pyrce-Jones. Calling the Reverend she suggested that Pete's band would make a good addition to the upcoming festivities. He agreed on principle, providing he could see them play first.

May 1957

To fulfil the Reverend Pyrce-Jone's condition and allow him to judge their suitability, The Quarry Men were invited to play a few numbers for the Youth Club Dances at St. Peters Youth Club. This was a wise precaution on the part of the Reverend considering that both Pete Shotton and John Lennon had been thrown out of the Sunday School because of their rebellious behavior. The Youth Club performances became popular and people started turning up just to hear them play. As their popularity increased John became more demanding, asking for a microphone so he could be heard better. When a microphone didn't materialize one evening as promised, John told the Quarry Men to pack up and left the hall without playing a note. Colin also recalls a gig "*somewhere around*

Penny Lane, an annual dance for the Vespa Scooter Club. Something like that.[38]" Unfortunately no documentary evidence of these, John Lennon's earliest public performances, exists.

In the summer John approached the new headmaster at Quarry Bank, William Pobjoy, about the possibility of his group playing at the school sixth form dances. Mr Pobjoy had arrived at Quarry Bank the year before and realized that he had a problem with John Lennon. After talking to John, Mr. Pobjoy decided to try and get John to channel his energies into things that interested him— music and art. So following John's request he "booked" the Quarry Men to play for the sixth-form dance at the end of the school year.

> *"John was a boy of great talent. Skiffle was not his main interest at that time. It was a strong interest (but not his main one). I asked him to write out for me what his principal interests were and he began with salmon fishing. In those days he hadn't thought of making money from it (skiffle). For example he came to me and asked permission to play with The Quarry Men in the interval of the sixth form dance. I said I'd think about it and reluctantly agreed. But it never occurred to him to ask for money.*[39]"

Most schoolboy skiffle groups of the time were playing in front of easy, friendly audiences comprised of friends at local church halls and school dances. In this respect The Quarry Men were no different than any other of the numerous bands that had arisen following the explosion of skiffle on the British cultural scene. Perhaps one factor that lead them along on the first steps to success was the enterprising spirit of Nigel Walley, for it was through Nigel that they took their first forays away from the church/school circuit.

After leaving school Nigel started working as an Assistant Pro at a local Golf Club, Lee Park, also known as the Childwall Golf Course. One of his first successes was to secure the group a booking to play at a Golf Club evening function. According to Len Garry, the group all wore large check shirts with white tassles, and were joined for the first time by their friend John "Duff" Lowe on piano— solely due to the fact that there was a piano available on the stage.

However Rod Davis disputes this[40]. Davis recalls playing the Childwall Golf Course gig, but says he didn't meet John Lowe until 1984. Davis is also adamant that the group did not wear any tasseled check shirts, but black jeans and white shirts. This caused Rod much worry because his parents didn't allow him to wear jeans and he had to buy a second hand pair from a friend. However, both agree that official payment for the evening's work was in the form of a good hot meal from the Golf Club dining room. A hat was passed around at the end of the set which resulted in enough cash for the boys to think that they could actually get paid to play, rather than just do it for fun.

As assistant Golf Pro, Nigel also caddied for several prominent local business men and used the conversations on the links to leverage opportunities for his charges. A regular player at the club was local doctor, Dr. Sytner, father of Alan Sytner owner of the newly opened Cavern club. Through this connection, Nigel Walley procured a booking for The Quarry Men to play a session at the Cavern's skiffle-night in the upcoming August.

Over in Speke, thanks to constant practice, 14 year old George Harrison's skill on the guitar had now surpassed that of his brother and the capabilities of his cheap guitar. Once more George's mother was instrumental in furthering her youngest son's ambitions and scrapped together enough money to buy a £30 Hofner President cutaway semi-acoustic guitar. George learnt to play his new guitar by constantly listening to a collection of Buddy Holly records owned by his friend Tony Bramwell. He also wired it to a crude amplifier mounted on an unpainted chipboard speaker cabinet. It wasn't pretty but it was effective.

Occasionally George would ask the advice of his friend Paul, who had a greater theoretical understanding of music. They began to practice at both McCartney and Harrison households, swapping ideas and discussing the merits of their various musical heroes. During the summer break they even packed their guitars for a three week hiking trip along the south coast of England, often sleeping rough on beaches to save a few shillings. On the return to school the afternoon practice sessions would continue, as both boys began to truant even more. This was not unexpected for George, but somewhat shocking for A-stream class captain McCartney.

June 1957

With his new guitar in hand, George Harrison was quicker in securing a paying audience than The Quarry Men had been. In early June George founded his own group called "The Rebels" and secured a gig at the local British Legion club in Speke.

This gig was to be the one and only appearance by "The Rebels" whose line up consisted of George Harrison, his brother Pete, and friend Arthur Kelly, all with guitars and *"one or two other friends*[41]*"* yet to be identified, who provided a rhythm section with the obligatory tea-chest bass (covered in wallpaper that was decorated with gnomes) and mouth-organ. In fact the whole gig came about by chance. George and his friends had been playing around with their new instruments at Arthur Kelly's house when they received a call from the promoter at the local Legion club offering them an audition.

Hastily christening the band and painting "Rebels" across the front of the tea chest bass, they arrived at the hall to await their promised audition. As show time approached the scheduled band failed to appear and "The Rebels" were co-opted onto the stage to provide the evening's entertainment. For this they received 10 shillings each. Unfortunately "The Rebels" knew precisely two songs, but the promoter didn't seem to mind too much that his new group kept repeating the same tunes.

George was so enthused about his first stage experience that on the following Monday morning he spent the whole bus ride to school telling his friend, Paul McCartney, about it.

As their first step on the road to becoming a paid "professional" group, The Quarry Men entered the local round of the Carrol Levis "Discoveries" talent search. Levis was the producer of a top TV talent show and held "heats" in most provincial cities. The winners of the heats progressed to regional "finals" with a vague hope of securing a two-minute TV slot. The Quarry Men entered the heat held on Sunday the 9th of June 1957 at the Liverpool Empire. With little to distinguish them from any other of the numerous skiffle groups that entered, they failed miserably. An often-repeated tale is that the winner of the heat was a group named The Sunnysiders with a memorable gimmick, a midget bass player named Nicky Cuff, who happened to be a work mate of Colin Hanton's. The surviving members of the Quarry Men recall that "*a group from North Wales who had a coach load of supporters who clapped loudest and thus won*[42]" beat them

Their next gig turned out to be more promising, for they had secured their first real paid engagement. The occasion was the 750th Anniversary of the granting of Liverpool's Royal Charter, granted by King John in the 1200s.** Hundreds of street parties were being held all over the city, with food, dancing and music. The Quarry Men had been booked to provide the music for the celebrations in Rosebery Street. The booking had come about because the organizer of the Rosebery Street celebrations, a Majorie Roberts, had a son, Charlie, who was friendly with Quarry Men drummer Colin Hanton.

The Quarry Men's "stage" on this auspicious 22nd July was the back of a local coal merchant's wagon. The wagon was provided by the resident of number 76 who also supplied the "sound system," a microphone wired in through an old radio set that acted as a tiny, and tinny, amplifier.

The Quarry Men played two sets during the day's festivities. During which John announced his arrival on the "professional" stage by acting "*cocky, as if he knew he was good, winking at the girls as he played and showing a dry sense of humor.*[43]" John's attitude soon attracted the attention of not only the local girls but also the members of a local gang from neighboring Hatherley Street who were soon heard to be muttering threats to "*get that Lennon.*[44]"

After the gig Mrs. Roberts provided shelter for the group in

** *Several sources, including John, say it was an "Empire Day" celebration. However the two events were different and held at different times of the year*

her house (Number 84). She calmly served the boys with tea and refreshments while they awaited a Police escort. So, in a strange foreshadowing of the events of Beatlemania many years later, John Lennon and his group were escorted to their transport, in this case the local bus, by the police called in for their own protection. Although in this case it was a single policeman rather than the ring of police that would be required in later years.

Roseberry Street won an award that day from the local Liverpool Echo newspaper for the best decorated street. To celebrate they held another street party, but the Quarry Men were not invited back, their place being taken by the Merseysippi Jazz band.

In her book[45] John's half-sister Julia Bird claimed that the boys all wore different colored shirts and called themselves "Johnny & The Rainbows" for this gig but the name "Quarry Men" can clearly be seen "painted"♣ on Colin Hanton's drums in the photo taken by Charles Roberts that day.

The day's events were far from over. According to Len Garry, The Quarry Men's bass player at the time, at a party later in the evening, John and Pete Shotton, who were both possibly drunk, got into an argument which only ended when John broke the washboard over his best friends head*! Shotton replaced the washboard but only played one more gig with The Quarry Men, at the St Peters church fete later that month. According to Davis the incident happened after the St. Peter's fete at a private party

---

♣   *The name Quarry Men wasn't painted on as generally believed, but cut out from black paper, taped onto the drum face and replaced when they fell off or faded.*

*   *According to Goldman in THE LIVES OF JOHN LENNON the argument was between Pete Shotton & Colin Hanton on stage at the "Wilson Hall". Pete complained that the rhythm of Colin's drums on ALL SHOOK UP didn't match the one John was tapping out with his foot. The fight lead to a "him or me" type showdown to which John replied that "drums are better than washboards" and promptly broke the washboard over Shotton's head. However this version of the story is not supported by any other source*

held at a relative of drummer Colin Hanton's[46] and Pete never picked up the washboard again. Pete Shotton himself places the "argument" at a wedding reception in Toxteth in the August. *"John and I were sat on the floor at the end of the party surrounded by our instruments and empty beer bottles. I wanted to leave, my contribution was totally non-musical. I plucked up the courage to say I was leaving, he* (John) *suddenly picked up the washboard and hit me over the head with it and said 'That takes care of that problem, doesn't it?'*"[47]

His first paid gig was not the only landmark event in John Lennon's life that June. The stage was also set for another life-change that would profoundly effect John and the development of the group that eventually became The Beatles.

Realizing that John's talents lay outside the mainstream classifications of the British education system, Quarry Bank headmaster, William Pobjoy, arranged for John to interview for Liverpool's art college with the principal, Mr. Stevenson . For once John was on his best behavior and managed to secure a place at the college. John was always grateful to Mr Pobjoy for getting him into Art School.

Many years later, replying to a fan letter from a pupil at Quarry Bank he wrote *"Remember me to anyone who is still there, even to Pobjoy. After all it was he who got me into Art School so I could fail there too, and I can never thank him enough."*

July 1957

The 6th July 1957 is arguably the most important date in the early story of The Beatles[•]. This day above all others has probably been discussed and investigated to a greater depth—even being worthy of a book dedicated to this day alone[α].

- [•] Ranked #12 in "The 100 Greatest Moments in Rock 'n' Roll"—*Entertainment Weekly #487 dated May 28th 1999.*
- [α] O'Donnell, Jim. THE DAY JOHN MET PAUL. Penguin. 1996. New York. ISBN 0-14-025301-7

For this was the day that John Lennon met Paul McCartney. Although according to at least one researcher[48] John and Paul had already met outside of a local "chippy" (fish and chip shop) in the late spring of 1957. They allegedly greeted each other as mutual friends of Ivan Vaughan but didn't stop to have a conversation. This incident is not backed up by any other account, nor any published interviews.

However in a TV interview Paul did acknowledge that he already knew who John was, prior to the fateful day they were introduced. "*I had seen John around on the local buses. He was a Ted and I thought he looked cool, but didn't speak to him until Ivy* (Ivan Vaughn) *introduced us.*"[49]

The big event in Woolton each summer was a garden fete and "Rose Queen" procession organized by St. Peter's parish church. In another example of Beatles coincidence, it was discovered in the late 1980s, that a gravestone in the churchyard at St. Peter's carried the name "Eleanor Rigby".

The fete planned for July 6th 1957 made a break from tradition in that "*for the first time the teenagers of the parish were to be catered for. (The) Lennon boy had been asked to bring his group, The Quarry Men, to take part in the procession and to perform afterwards at the fete*[50]". The invitation had come as a direct result of Pete Shotton's mother's suggestion to the Reverend Pryce-Jones the previous month.

Early on the Saturday afternoon (around 1 pm according to Len Garry's account) The Quarry Men climbed aboard a gaily decked coal merchant's wagon driven by 17 year old Doug Chadwick. It had been decided that their float should bring up the rear of the procession *to "allay any clash of rhythms with the band of The Cheshire Yeomanry* (who led the parade).[51]" In between came the floats of local organizations and traders. The centerpiece being the float carrying the throne of the newly crowned 13 year-old Rose Queen, a Miss Sally Wright.

Garry recalls "*Apparently we were to perform on five occasions that day. Firstly on the float, then twice in the afternoon at 4.15pm in* the church field and then twice in the church hall starting at 8pm that evening"[52]

Songs planned for the back of the wagon performance included WORRIED MAN BLUES, MAGGIE MAE, RAILROAD BILL and MIDNIGHT SPECIAL.

Church Road has a gradient of about 1:4 and, given their precarious position, The Quarry Men decided not to start playing until they reached an even gradient. As they reached level ground John launched into his rendition of MIDNIGHT SPECIAL. The rest of the set followed as the procession wound its way down that almost equally steep King's Drive, past the home of Quarry Man Rod Davis at number129, and then along Hunt's Cross Avenue. About half way around the group became worried about losing their balance and sat down. John sat on the edge of the wagon with his legs swung over the side as he continued to play. The procession arrived back at the church around 2.50pm.

The Quarry Men stored their instruments in the Scout Hut and joined in the festivities as The Rose Queen was officially crowned and the fete opened.

Having amused themselves at the various sideshows, the boys returned to the Scout Hut at 4.00pm as the brass band was finishing up its performance. The Quarry Men set up their instruments on the small semi-permanent platform constructed from artificial composite walling stones.

As can be seen in the famous photograph taken that day by fellow Quarry Bank pupil Geoff Rhind, John was at the microphone, center stage and right at the front. Len Garry was placed on his left and Eric Griffiths on his right. Rod Davis, Colin Hanton & Pete Shotton were arranged behind John.

Rather than use his usual introductory quips, John opened the set by launching straight into ALL SHOOK UP and BLUE SUEDE SHOES. Len Garry remarks that there was a noticeable "*change in Lennon's level of enthusiasm as he rasped these songs*[53]" in comparison to the way he'd performed the standard skiffle numbers earlier in the day.

The rock 'n' roll numbers were followed by a rendition of

MAGGIE MAE, a song about a Liverpool prostitute, cheekily dedicated by John *"to Pricey"*, the vicar of St Peter's Pryce-Jones.

During the afternoon session John's aunt and guardian, Mimi Smith, was taking refreshments in the tea tent when the kids started rushing out of the tent towards the band stand. Looking out to see what was happening Mimi was horrified to see John on stage.

> *"John saw me standing there. He started making up words about me in the song he was singing 'Mimi's coming, Oh, oh, Mimi's coming down the path.'"*[54]

John's talent for improvisation was not limited to lyrics about his aunt. The Quarry Men also played their usual arrangement of the Del Vikings' hit COME GO WITH ME. On the original the lead sings "Love, love me darlin'. Come and go with me, Please don't send me, way beyond the sea." Unable to make out the last phrase John had slotted in what he thought was a typical American word. The result was *"Come, come, come go with me. Down to the penitentiary."*

John wound up the first afternoon session at around 5pm with THAT'LL BE THE DAY.

The Quarry Men brought a large influx of teenagers into Woolton to see the parade. At the back of the crowd during the afternoon performance had stood John's friend and neighbor, Ivan Vaughan with his school friend, Paul McCartney. Ivan, Paul's classmate at the Institute, had asked him over. *"to see the band he sometimes played in, The Quarry Men, and to meet its leader, a 'great fellow' by the name of John Lennon"*.[55]

It appears that Paul McCartney wasn't initially impressed with John Lennon's guitar playing. He was, however, impressed by John's improvisation of slotting in words from blues songs, like "penitentiary," when he didn't know the correct lyrics.

> *"There was one particular guy at the front that had a checked shirt, greased back hair, side boards—looking pretty cool. He was playing one of those cheap mail-order guitars,*

guaranteed not to crack. But he was making a good job of it and I remember being quite impressed.[56]"

Following a brief performance by the local Police dogs, The Quarry Men returned to the outdoor stage at around 5.30pm and according to Len Garry *"switched onto automatic pilot, with hardly any enthusiasm we dutifully played and sang our way through our skiffle repertoire . . . by 6.20pm we had had enough.*[57]"

According to Garry, Paul McCartney missed this second performance as he'd cycled back to 20 Forthilin Road to collect his guitar. As Paul would have needed a guitar stringed for a left-handed player in order to show any level of proficiency. However this contradicts events as later recalled by Paul[58] and confirmed by other members of the Quarry Men[59], that he played left handed on a right handed guitar, possibly Eric Griffiths', playing the chords upside down.

At around 6.45pm the group moved over to the back of the church hall at the opposite end from the stage were they were due to perform at 8.45pm and 10.00pm following The George Edwards Band.

At around 7.00pm Paul McCartney entered the hall with Ivan Vaughn. Ivan introduced him to the rest of the group leaving John till last. John's response on being introduced to Paul was a simple "Hi" nothing more. John was busy tuning his guitar still using banjo chords and practically ignored Paul until McCartney offered to give him a hand tuning his guitar the correct way. John responded to Paul's low-key offer of help and as Paul re-tuned John's guitar to the correct chords the conversation drifted to favorite artists. Paul's mention of Elvis, Eddie Cochran, Gene Vincent and Little Richard further prompted Lennon's interest.

Pete Shotton recalls that Paul's' ability to retune the guitars also impressed John, although he didn't show it at the time. At this point neither John, nor Eric Griffiths had learnt how to tune their instruments and used to pay *"a fellow in King's Drive"*[60] to do it for them.

With some encouragement from Ivan, Paul launched into his

party piece Little Richard impersonation and sang LONG TALL SALLY. Asked by John if he knew anything else Paul admitted to knowing all the words to Eddie Cochran's TWENTY FLIGHT ROCK and proceeded to demonstrate by playing the whole song. Despite it now being recognized as a classic rock tune, at this point TWENTY FLIGHT ROCK was an obscure track. It's probable that Paul and John first encountered it during Cochran's cameo performance in the 1956 movie "The Girl Can't Help It." However it was never released as a single in the UK or the US, being ignored by Cochran's record company for years. It didn't get much, if any, radio play, and Cochran didn't have his first UK hit until November 1958. So why would Paul choose this song to learn, and where would he hear it often enough to learn the lyrics? This either serves as a perfect example of how far ahead of the times musically, and in terms of awareness of US music, Paul, John and the rest of the Quarry Men were. Or, it may be an indication of how one person's faulty memory through repeated telling gets accepted as the norm and becomes adopted as the truth, even by those involved.

In fact neither Colin nor Rod has any clear recollection of Paul's momentous meeting with John, nor of hearing anyone, let alone Paul, play TWENTY FLIGHT ROCK that evening. Eric recalls Paul's meeting with John but says the first time he heard Paul play the Eddie Cochran song was later at Paul's house.

Following his "performance", Paul then sat down with a piece of paper and pencil and drew out some bar chords for John. What exactly Paul wrote for John is disputed and no surviving record exists. Some accounts suggest that Paul wrote the lyrics to TWENTY FLIGHT ROCK, others that it was BE-BOP-A LULA. It's also been suggested that Paul told John that he was singing the wrong lyrics to COME GO WITH ME and wrote out a correct set of lyrics for John to learn. Of all the possible scenarios, this later one seems the most likely.

Paul's recollection of this momentous occasion is somewhat briefer than other accounts; he recalled:

> "*this beery old man getting nearer and breathing down my neck as I was playing. It was John.... I showed him a few more chords he didn't know, then I left. I felt I'd made a good impression.*"

Paul's remark about John's beery breath has been taken by many researchers to indicate that John was drunk that day. Quarry Men Len Garry and Pete Shotton both disagree. Pete Shotton recalls "*He didn't have enough money to get drunk, even if we did like the stuff. We were drunk at the Rosebery Street celebration but I don't remember John being drunk on the day of the fete.*[61]"

The Quarry Men returned to the stage at 8.45pm refreshed. Len Garry noticed that "*meeting Paul had wetted his (John's) appetite. He seemed to have a new sparkle, as though he'd had an injection of renewed optimism and enthusiasm.*"

The Quarry Men completed 14 songs split between the two sessions that evening. The first session included ALL SHOOK UP, BE BOPA LULA, BLUE SUEDE SHOES, FREIGHT TRAIN, HOUND DOG, MAGGIE MAE and RAILROAD BILL.

The second session was BABY LET'S PLAY HOUSE, PUTTIN' ON THE STYLE, JAILHOUSE ROCK, WORRIED MAN BLUES, CUMBERLAND GAP, MIDNIGHT SPECIAL and finished at around 10.30pm with the Del Viking's COME GO WITH ME. At least two songs from this evening session "PUTTIN' ON THE STYLE" and "BABY LET'S PLAY HOUSE." were caught by St Peter's Youth Club member Bob Molyneux, on an amateur reel-to-reel tape and were auctioned at Sotheby's in 1994 for around $100,000.

The day's work may have been over but the leader of The Quarry Men faced an important decision.

Pete Shotton[62] recalls that "(Following the gig) *John and I walked home alone and John said to me 'What do you think of him (Paul)?' I said 'I like him.' And he said 'What about asking him to join the band then?' so I said 'Well if he wants to it's OK with me.*"

John later recalled "*I was the singer and the leader and I made the decision whether to have him in the group or not. Was it the right thing to do to have someone who was better than the guys I already had, obviously. And that decision was to let Paul in to make the group stronger. I turned round to him right there on our first meeting and said 'Do you want to join the group?' And I think he said 'Yes' the next day.[63]"

John's version of events is slightly at odds with other accounts from both Pete Shotton and Paul McCartney, for although the St. Peter's fete marked Pete's last appearance with The Quarry Men, (after the earlier washboard incident, Pete had decided he'd had enough, he remained John's closest and most loyal friend,) Pete still had one vital role to play in the future of The Quarry Men.

Around the 20th of July Paul McCartney had cycled over to see Ivan Vaughan but he wasn't at home. Pete Shotton had left his house en-route to see John when he saw Paul turning the corner of Linkstor Road and Vale Road. Pete called to Paul and told him "*John and I have been talking it over and we both agreed that we'd like to ask you if you wanted to join the group.*" Paul thought for a few moments then with a sudden "*OK then. See you*" he cycled off.[64]

So with a simple "OK" the foundation for the greatest songwriting team in popular music was laid.

August 1957

On August 7th 1957, John Lennon stepped onto the stage at The Cavern for his first documented appearance at the club. According to Rod Davis the Quarry Men had played the club a few times early on an unbilled basis[65]. This occasion was the first time that they'd been mentioned in the Cavern's advertising published in the Liverpool Echo. Considering the later relationship between The Beatles and the famous venue in Mathew Street, this debut was less than auspicious.

The gig had been arranged by Nigel Walley through his golf club connections and Alan Sytner had reluctantly squeezed the schoolboy group onto the bill for the Wednesday skiffle night session. Sytner's rules of engagement were simple. If it was skiffle night—you played skiffle and nothing else, because that's what the audience had come to hear.

Of course for John Lennon, rules were made to be broken, or at least bent a little. The Quarry Men, without their newest member Paul McCartney who was away at a Boy Scout camp, started their set with their standard skiffle routine. But John was itching to play rock 'n' roll. Something, according to Davis, that he'd tried on previous occasions and been prevented by arguments from the banjo player. However on this occasion The Quarry Men were without Rod as he was on a family vacation on France. Unchallenged John proudly introduced *"two new skiffle numbers"* to their set, BLUE SUEDE SHOES and HOUND DOG.

Alan Sytner was less than amused and a hastily written note was passed on stage from the club owner telling Mr. Lennon and his group to *"Cut out the bloody rock."*[66] His view of their overall performance was equally dismissive. *"They went down all right, but it was hardly a discerning audience. I thought they were pretty useless, just a bunch of kids going through their apprenticeship.*[67]*"*

Shortly after The Quarry Men's Cavern gig, their erstwhile member Paul McCartney made his debut on the public stage. On a family vacation to Butlin's Holiday Camp in Filey, Yorkshire, Paul and his younger brother Mike entered a "National" talent contest organized and sponsored by "The People" newspaper.

The boys were encouraged to enter by their cousin Elizabeth and her husband, Mike, who were both Red Coats at the camp. Entering as "The McCartney Brothers" the duo sang a couple of numbers but failed to qualify for the next round. There is some disagreement as to what exactly was performed. According to some accounts[68] they first sang the Everly Brother's BYE BYE LOVE as a duet, followed by Paul's solo rendition of Little Richard's LONG TALL SALLY. Unfortunately Mike's nerves got the better of him as at the conclusion of Paul's song he rushed off-stage to throw up in the nearest fire bucket. As he was just recovering from a broken arm and, by Paul's own account, "looked very pale" it may have been all too much for him. But, it would not have mattered even if their performance had been perfect. There was no way they could progress to the next round as the contest rules stated that all contestants had to be over 16 years of age[69].

Back in Liverpool various members of The Quarry Men were heading for life changing decisions as the new school year started.

Rod Davis decided to stay on at Quarry Bank and enter the sixth form in order to study for his A-levels, a necessary requirement for University entrance. As a consequence he *"drifted out of the Quarrymen . . . then bought a guitar and became part of a jazz trio at Quarry Bank, piano, guitar and drums.*[70]*"*

Eric Griffiths left school and started as an apprentice engineer with local aircraft engine manufacturers Napier. As Eric started his apprenticeship, so drummer Colin Hanton neared completion of his.

John's friend Pete Shotton entered the Police Training School.

The old gang was starting to break-up. Although they all still lived close to one another, the daily contact at Quarry Bank school was no more.

September 1957

John was not isolated from these changes, for he too started a new phase in his life. Liverpool Art College.

As the Liverpool Art College shared the same physical building with the Liverpool Institute, the two being connected by a corridor that provided easy access between them, John now exchanged daily contact with his Quarry Bank crowd for daily contact with Liverpool Institute attendee, and new group member, Paul McCartney and his "tag along" chum, George Harrison.

Attendance at the Art College also had one other major impact on John Lennon, for here he met the one person who, arguably, had the greatest impact on his life. Stuart Sutcliffe.

Although only 4 months older than John, Stuart was a couple of years ahead of him at the art college due to his natural talent for painting. Stuart's family was from an entirely different background to John's and it seems strange on the surface that they should be such good friends.

Born in Scotland on 23rd June 1940, Stuart moved to the Liverpool area with his family in 1943 when his father was relocated as an "essential war worker" at the shipyard in nearby Birkenhead. After the war his father returned to the Merchant Navy, like John's father, and spent most of the subsequent years away from the family. As a consequence Stuart and his younger sisters were raised, almost single handedly by his mother Milli, a school teacher and political activist.

The Sutcliffe house was always full of books, paintings and music. Both parents had studied the piano and still played, but painting was Stuart's passion even from an early age. It was a teacher at Prescott Grammar School, a Mr. Walters, who first recognized his talent and gave him encouragement. So much so that he had earned enough credit to be able to enroll in The Liverpool Art College two years earlier than normal.

Co-incidentally the year was 1956 and, along with many others, Stuart had also discovered rock n roll in general and Elvis in particular. While painting continued to be Stuart's passion, Elvis was now his own personal God.

As the Sutcliffe's technically lived outside the city boundaries of Liverpool, in the suburb of Huyton, he was not given several of the living expense grants available to other students. In order to cut down the costs of traveling to and from the College each day, Stuart rented a succession of small apartments, which over the coming years, would resound to the sounds of guitars.

Despite their apparent differences John and Stuart formed an almost immediate bond. John admired Stuart's sense of style, his knowledge of art and the fact that he was more "worldly." While in John, Stuart seemed to sense someone who reflected his own inner rebellious wishes. Being different was a quality much admired by Stuart, and John was certainly different.

Their dress style seemed to complement their characters, too. John was dressed for attention in tight "drainies" (drainpipe jeans with narrowed legs) and a long flocked black coat that he wore with "*a swagger and self assurance camouflaging his insecurities.*[71]" While Stuart dressed in an individual style, he did so for himself. John was overtly anarchic while Stuart displayed his "anarchy" through his paintings, pushing the boundaries of his craft, in a way that can now be seen to be way ahead of its time.

It also helped that Stuart was on the Student Union Committee by this time and would have been seen by John as someone who could be in a position to give his group some work at the college dances. They were introduced by a mutual friend, Bill Harry, who would later found the Mersey Beat newspaper.

It wasn't long before the three new friends would escape the confines of the College to while way hours at the nearby "Cracke" pub, where they would, as all students did, complain about the lectures. But they would also talk about Buddy Holly, Elvis and rock 'n' roll while Stuart introduced them to painters such as Amedo Modigilani and poets such as Arthur Rimbaud.

October 1957

Although he had yet to play a single note in public with The Quarry Men, Paul had already become a significant influence on the remaining members. By now rehearsals had switched to the McCartney's front room in Forthlin Road.

In mid October John, Len Garry, Eric Griffiths, Nigel Walley and Paul met to rehearse and discuss the upcoming gig scheduled for the 18th. Paul suggested that The Quarry Men "dress it up a bit" by wearing long white jackets and present a smarter image on stage.

Paul had a supporter in Nigel Walley, who as their nominal "manager" had tried to smarten them up as much as possible for the Golf Club gig earlier in the year.

They reached a compromise that meant the band would have a more "together" look. Paul and John would wear the jackets while the rest of the group would wear white shirts and black string ties.

Nearly three months after agreeing to join the group, Paul McCartney finally made his debut as a member of The Quarry Men on 18th October at the New Clubmoor Hall, a Conservative Club in Norris Green. The Quarry Men were booked by local promoter Charlie McBain (Who also owned and ran the Wilson

Hall in Garston which was actually closer to where most of the group lived.) Entrance fee was 3 shillings.

The Quarry Men were the second band on that night, scheduled to be on-stage at 9.00pm. The band assembled backstage at around 7.50 after a two bus journey to the club. They spent the time before going on-stage tuning their instruments, messing about and consuming a fair amount of alcohol and cigarettes.

At the appointed hour they climbed on the low stage close to the crowd of around 100 people, mainly in their late teens and early twenties. On stage Len Garry (bass) was at the back, Paul (guitar) to his right, John (guitar) to his left. Eric Griffiths (guitar) was placed far left and Colin Hanton (drums) on the far right. Even though this was his first gig with the group, Paul had naturally taken the front and center position alongside John. As a result of the earlier compromise they all wore matching outfits with long sleeved cowboy shirts, black string ties and black trousers. John and Paul also donned the much discussed white jackets.

The group had prepared a play list of around 20 songs, leading off with LONG TALL SALLY (sung by Paul). It got such a good reaction that they hastily rearranged the play list to include more Little Richard songs for Paul to sing. John followed Paul with a rendition of ALL SHOOK UP which he introduced by announcing to the audience that *"for the next number I'll just have to put on my Elvis wig."*[72] Even at this early stage John's repartee with the audience was highly unusual as very few bands ever bothered to speak to the audience—they just came on and played.

Paul then started on his much rehearsed party piece solo, GUITAR BOOGIE. Part way through he seemed to miss a few chords and it threw him. John realizing that Paul was in trouble brought the number to an end by quipping *"He's our new boy— He'll be alright given time."* John's use of humor covered what could have been an embarrassing incident for Paul. The group then settled in to play the rest of their set and received *"quite rousing applause. Probably not for our rendition of the songs, but more likely for the sheer cheekiness of that chap Lennon."*[73]

Some sources suggest that Paul's clumsiness was as a result of the fact that he had only just restringed his guitar to play it left handed. This seems unlikely as most of members of The Quarry Men remember him playing it "upside down" from the earliest rehearsals.

This gig is also significant in that it possibly marks the beginning of the Lennon-McCartney song writing team. It's generally agreed that it was after this gig that Paul first played John a song he'd written called I LOST MY LITTLE GIRL. As Paul recalls it was "*a funny little song based on three chords, G, G7 and C.*"[74] John was impressed enough to start working on his own songs.

Unfortunately for the Quarry Men the numerous other skiffle groups and burgeoning rock acts in Liverpool were fishing in the same well for inspiration. It wasn't too long before it was becoming difficult to tell the groups apart by their play lists. This was problem that Paul and John were determined to tackle.

> "*Our first thought was to search out for obscure B-sides, then the light bulb went off. If we wrote our own songs then nobody else could do them first. So we started writing to put one over on the other bands.*"[75]

November 1957

Although the exact date of the start of the Lennon-McCartney collaboration is difficult to pin down, there is no denying that by early November 1957 the two had started to work together on a regular basis.

Paul recalls "*We used to sag off school together and go back to my house because there was nobody home in the afternoons. We'd sit around smoking and talking and then we'd play a bit on my Dad's piano or on our guitars. We would try different songs that either of us knew. John would teach me the ones he knew, and I'd teach him the ones I knew. We began to write a lot of songs then like LOVE ME DO and TOO MUCH ABOUT SORROWS. There was a lot from then. About 100 that we never recorded.*"[76]

Perhaps the most remarkable thing about this period is not just the prolific number of songs, but the informal contract that the two teenagers arranged between themselves. Not all the songs were joint efforts. But they decided that no matter who the originator, every song would share a joint credit. It's interesting to note that even though Paul had known George longer and had already played around composing a few songs together•, this arrangement with John effectively froze him out of receiving any credit for his contributions for years to come. At this point George hadn't expressed any burning desire to be a song writer; that was to come much later.

The nascent song writing partnership of John and Paul recorded their compositions in a school exercise book**. Each new song would be started with the legend "Another Lennon-McCartney Original" scrawled across the top of the page.

It was very rare for them to compose a piece together from the start. The song writing sessions were generally "to polish off some songs they'd begun on their own. Starting a song may have meant having an idea for a melody, or arriving with an almost complete song which just needed the essential middle eight hook. It may also have meant coming up with a great title and a first line and needing help with a direction. Or, having heard a great new rock 'n' roll song and wanting to make a version that was all their own—from early on each song bore the distinctive signature of either John or Paul—they were markedly different in their approaches to songwriting."[77]

Charlie McBain who had booked The Quarry Men for the October 18th gig invited them back to play at his other venue, The Walton Hall in nearby Garston. Payment was to be £2.10s or 10 shillings for each band member.

McBain advertised the group on the gig posters as a "Rock 'N' Roll Skiffle Group," the first public acknowledgement that the group's repertoire was changing.

•   IN SPITE OF ALL THE DANGER and HEY DARLIN being two documented Harrison-McCartney collaborations from this period.

**   These priceless notebooks were lost in the sixties when Paul's long-term girlfriend Jane Asher accidentally threw them out whilst spring-cleaning their house.

Walton Hall was known more locally for its fist fights than for live music and The Quarry Men's support "act" for that November 7th gig was a juke box placed on the stage. Given the club's reputation, the boys didn't bother to dress up. Even this early on they went their own way, not always acting as promoters and managers expected.

Following the jukebox on stage The Quarry Men launched into their set with Paul taking the lead on TWENTY FLIGHT ROCK. Much to the boys disgust, the surly crowd continued to chat and ignore them, just as if the jukebox had still been on stage.

However when John moved to center stage, the chatting stopped as he launched into a powerful raspy nasal rendition of THAT'LL BE THE DAY. *"His stage presence seemed to carry us through,"* noted Len Garry.

The crowd won over, The Quarry Men completed their set and this time Paul's rendition of GUITAR BOOGIE was faultless.

The group's local reputation was starting to build as nine days later the boys found themselves playing a gig at the social club attached to the local abattoir in nearby Stanley.

The 23rd of November saw a return to the site of Paul's debut, The Clubmoor Hall. A photograph taken that night by local fan Leslie Kearney shows the lineup as John (vocals/guitar), Paul (vocals/guitar), Eric Griffiths (guitar), Colin Hanton (drums), Len Garry (tea chest bass).

Sometime during this month, The Quarry Men also performed at the regular Friday night dances at the Haig Dance Club on Haig Avenue across the Mersey in Moreton on the Wirral peninsular. Unfortunately, no documentary evidence of the exact dates of these first gigs outside the Liverpool city boundaries seems to exist.

December 1957

In early December 1957 a disenchanted drama student returned to Liverpool from the Royal Academy Of Dramatic Arts in London to rejoin the family furniture business, "I. Epstein & Sons" in Walton Road.

Born on 19th September 1934 into wealth and privilege Brian Epstein's childhood was very different from that of the four "boys" he would later groom for international stardom. The Epstein business was very successful and the family were affluent enough that Brian was raised by a nanny. He grew up under the watchful eye of his devoted mother, Queenie, for whom he could do no wrong.

He was educated at a series of high fee paying schools and did badly at all of them. In 1950 he dropped out of the education system at 16 and joined the family business. Two years later he was called up for his National Service and was stationed at Albany Barracks in London. Brian hated the discipline and army life so much that he never bothered collecting his pay. His stance and mannerisms soon brought him into conflict with the army authorities and he was discharged as "emotionally and mentally unfit" after 10 months.

Staying in London, Brian joined RADA in an attempt to launch a stage career. Here he learnt a lot about stage craft, presentation and how to manage a show—but little about acting. Disillusioned he returned to Liverpool.

As 23 year old Brian Epstein rejoined the family firm, the company was going through a period of expansion. One of the company stores had experimented with selling sheet music and instruments[*] from an annex under the name "North End Music Stores."

Around the time of Brian's return to the fold it had been decided to spin this venture off into a new store on Charlotte Street under the abbreviated "NEMS" name. Brian was installed as a director of the company and given the record department to run. He turned out to be an enthusiastic manager and the new venture returned a profit almost immediately.

At the nearby Art College, John and Stuart's friendship deepened, especially after Stuart and his flat mate Rod Murray

---

[*] *In another of those Beatles' "coincidences" it was from this store that Paul's father, Jim McCartney had purchased the family piano*

relocated to new "digs" at 9 Percy Street. Stuart decorated the flat in bold white and black patterns. It wasn't long before it became a hang out and a refuge for John. When Stuart spent some of his meager budget on a cheap record player and a collection of records that included *"every Elvis single available.*[78]" John became almost a permanent resident.

Not to be outdone, Rod Murray bought a tape recorder, forging Art College tutor Arthur Ballard's signature as the loan guarantor. Some evenings, after a session at The Cracke pub, Rod would record John and Stuart singing Elvis songs or copying routines from the anarchic comedy radio show "The Goons." Unfortunately these rare recordings, the first of John and Stuart together, have been lost.

It is also entirely feasible that The Quarry Men would join John for rehearsals at Percy Street.ƒ Rod Murray was a skiffle enthusiast and was in possession of his own washboard, it's therefore a reasonable assertion that he would have been interested in John's skiffle group and maybe even joined in with the rehearsals. If there were indeed "jam sessions" at Stuart's flat then he would also probably join the fun, making John's later invitation for him to join the group more understandable.

Rehearsals aside, The Quarry Men continued to play a number of local gigs that December, although only one can be accurately placed. On the 7th December they returned to Garston's Walton Hall. Among the crowd that night was Paul's young friend George Harrison getting his first glimpse• of his mate's group.[79] But it wasn't Paul that impressed young George, it was the strutting lead

---

ƒ   *None of the original Quarry Men have confirmed this, yet it seems logical conjecture.*

•• *This is probably the first recorded meeting between George and the members of The Quarry Men, however George's mother says that he first met the boys in a local chippy. Pete Shotton recalls them meeting George for the first time at the Harrison's house having gone there with Paul.*

singer, John Lennon. This was probably the start of George's well-documented "infatuation" with John that lasted for several years.

As well as playing at local dance halls, Nigel Walley also entered the group in numerous local talent shows, with them appearing at Locarno Ballroom in West Derby, the Pavilion Theatre on Lodge Lane, and the Rialto Ballroom in the city center on Upper Parliament Street. Colin remembers that the contest at the Locarno also included a section for male singers and Paul suggested to John that the two of them should enter. John's reaction was "*No way, we're not doing anything on our own. We're a group*[80]." Colin is of the impression that even at this stage Paul would have instantly dropped everyone else just for him and John to do something on their own.

Although the exact dates aren't recorded, it appears that the group also played a number of dates over that winter at Holyoake Hall on Smithdown Road, a few hundred yards away from the road junction known locally as "Penny Lane." Rod Davis also recalls "*The original skiffle group had played there at least once when I was with them.*[81]"

Despite all his previous efforts, Nigel Walley ended the year being gently leveraged out of his "management" role by Paul who couldn't understand why Nigel was receiving equal shares of any wages when he didn't play on stage.

By the end of 1957 The Quarry Men were a totally different ensemble than they had been at the start. They were well along the path from being a schoolboy skiffle band to becoming a nescient rock group.

PART THREE

"Tragedy & First Recording"—1958

January 1958

The Quarry Men continued to increase the number of gigs they played for Charlie McBain, almost becoming his regular house band. They started the year with a January 4th engagement at the New Clubmoor Hall. This was soon followed by a series of gigs at the Wilson Hall. At one point McBain did try to impose a female lead singer on the group, a girl called Pauline, who was with the Darktown Skiffle Group at the time. John and Paul wouldn't hear of it and made their views known to the promoter in no uncertain terms.

In late January the group returned to The Cavern for yet another skiffle night appearance. After their last encounter with club owner Alan Sytner, they stuck firmly to their skiffle repertoire. Sytner had gone beyond sending notes on stage to bands that broke the play list rules. He was now fining anyone who played rock numbers by withholding a portion of their meager wages for each violation. Although the gig passed without incident the January 24th date is significant in that it marked Paul McCartney's debut at The Cavern.

February 1958

The next major turning point in the development of The Quarry Men occurred on 6th February at a gig at the Wilson Hall in Garston. The evening set was nothing out of the ordinary and once more among the crowd was Paul's young friend George Harrison, who on this occasion he'd brought along his guitar.

After the gig George tagged along with the group as they caught the bus home. Paul had been working on John to take a listen to George's prowess on the guitar, "*I said I've got a friend who's pretty good*.⁸²" And now that he had a captive audience at the back of the upper deck of the bus, he persuaded George to try his party piece, a difficult guitar solo called "Raunchy."

John seemed suitably impressed as much by George's new guitar as by the skill of its owner, but felt George was still too young to join the group. However he conceded that George could fill in whenever Eric Griffiths was unavailable.

The location of this audition is much debated. The "back of the bus" story is the one most often told by both McCartney and Harrison. However others place the audition at a club called "The Morgue" in late '57. But, "The Morgue" didn't open until March 1958 by which time Quarry Men rehearsals had switched to the Harrison household on occasion, which suggests that George was already a member of the group by then.

March 1958

Perhaps one of the most pivotal events in the musical growth of John Lennon and Paul McCartney was the March 2nd showing of the ATV variety show "*Sunday Night At The London Palladium.*" The special guest artist was Buddy Holly & The Crickets, newly arrived in England and at the start of a countrywide tour. Among the TV audience was John, who gaped at Buddy's Fendor Stratocaster guitar, the first he'd ever seen. Many years later John would tell a fan that seeing the sheer number of sounds that Holly could produce from just three chords convinced John that he too could possibly write music** ⁸³. Paul would later say that he acquired his technical "info" as a rock 'n' roll guitar player by watching

---

**   *John also told the same fan that he believed that he was "the reincarnation of Buddy Holly."*

Buddy's performance and studying how he performed PEGGY SUE.[84]

The Holly influence was not restricted to just a TV show, for on March 20th Buddy Holly and his Crickets arrived in Liverpool for two shows at the Philharmonic Hall. Among the audience were Paul McCartney and John Lennon.

Paul recalls *"we loved his (Holly's) vocal sound and we loved his guitar playing and the fact that he wrote his own stuff. That's what turned us on."*[85]

John was entranced by this singer who wore his glasses on stage. Suddenly it was hip to be a rocker and wear spectacles. John started to feel less self-conscious and began to occasionally wear his thick black glasses on-stage and off. John became so enamoured of Buddy and The Crickets that he wrote a fan letter to Cricket drummer Jerry Allison's mother asking how Jerry and Buddy had formed The Crickets and asking advice on how his own band could "breakthrough" the same way Jerry's band had.[86]

Around this time The Quarry Men made an abortive attempt to break into local TV, going for an audition to the ABC TV studios in Manchester 35 miles away. The exact date isn't recorded and they didn't get through the audition, although both Colin and Eric recall the journey and their shock at finding out how expensive that train tickets were.

The first successful move for The Quarry Men away from the circuit of halls managed by Charlie McBain came in mid March with the opening of a new club called "The Morgue."

The Morgue was owned and operated by local teenager Alan Caldwell in the cellar of an old semi-derelict Victorian house at 25 Oakhill Broadgreen. Caldwell had aspirations to be a big rock star and his parents not only supported his dreams but actively encouraged them. In fact his mother even acted as his agent under the name "Downbeat Promotions." Caldwell saw the need for a purpose built venue for the growing number of Liverpool bands, one that wasn't owned and operated by the traditional dance hall promoters who didn't really understand what rock 'n' roll was about.

The Quarry Men were one on the groups invited to play on the March 13th opening night. Also among the acts was a solo singer called "Paul Rodgers" who's path would intersect with The Beatles in later years. "Paul Rodgers" was in fact Paul Murphy who eventually moved to Hamburg as A&R Manager for Polydor Records and it was Murphy who eventually purchased The Beatles early Hamburg tapes.

The group played at least two more gigs at The Morgue before it was closed down by the Police in early April due to overcrowding and "lack of proper facilities" such as restrooms and fire escapes.

Over the course of the of these gigs a rare McCartney—Harrison[∂] composition IN SPITE OF ALL THE DANGER was added to the group's repertoire, even though George wasn't a full member of the group as yet. Also introduced around this time was a McCartney penned instrumental called CATSWALK**.

Over this period George's stand-in gigs became more frequent until it reached the point that Eric Griffiths was effectively frozen out of the group. In yet another display of poor interpersonal relationships, Eric found out the hard way. A rehearsal was underway at the McCartney home which Eric hadn't been informed of. When word reached him, he telephoned to find out what was happening only to be bluntly told that The Quarry Men no longer required his services. Once again to avoid any confrontation, John persuaded Eric's best friend, Colin, that he should be the one to break the news The line up was now: John Lennon, Paul McCartney, George Harrison, Len Garry and Colin Hanton.

June 1958

The period between George joining the Quarry Men in late March and the end of June 1958 appears to have been one

---

[∂] *Although primarily a Paul composition, George created the guitar solo on the track and was given equal credit. In the Beatles Anthology video George refers to the track as "one of Paul's."*

** *Later recorded by skiffle pioneer Chris Barber under the title "Catcall."*

of little activity. No notable gigs or incidents have ever been documented to cover this period. In fact for most of the year the group was dormant and returned to playing the occasional party or wedding.

By the end of June they were auditioning for new dance club promoters including one at The Lowlands Club, Hyman's Green, West Derby but they failed to secure any bookings.

It was probably during this lull in the group's activities that George began his first serious relationship. He had fallen for a *"bright and wildly attractive girl named Ruth Morrison."*[87] George's relationship with Ruth would take on a pivotal role in the development of the group within the next 12 months

July 1958

The events of 15th July 1958 would scar the psyche of The Quarry Men's leader for the rest of his life. The tragedy that befell John Lennon that day would shape his behavior for the rest of his adult life and to a large extent influence the cynical approach to life that would forever mark him as "the cheeky one."

The Quarry Men's recently departed manger Nigel Walley called round to Mendips to talk to John, who was out at his mother's house. As it turned out Nigel found John's mother, Julia, outside Mendips talking to Mimi. Engaged in casual conversation, Nigel walked Julia part of the way home along Menlove Avenue. They parted and Julia crossed the road into the path of a car and was killed instantly. Her body was taken to Sefton General Hospital. The 17 year old John was at her house in Blomfield Road with her common-law husband John Dykins when police arrived to break the news.

The car was driven by an off-duty policeman (who John always swore was drunk, although that was never raised at the time) and who, despite Nigel Walley's eyewitness account, was acquitted. The shocked and distressed Nigel left Liverpool shortly after the court case. John retracted into a world of silence during the court case—knowing that he had been abandoned for the final time.

> "I lost her twice. Once as a five year old, when I moved in with my Auntie. And once again at 15* when she actually physically died.⁸⁸"

Prophetically a few month's earlier John had remarked to Paul about his behavior and asked *"How can you act so normal with your Mother dead? If anything like that happened to me, I'd go off my head."*— He kept good his promise—there was no limit to his anger and grief. He became meaner than ever and kept himself in a pain killing stupor of alcohol. His moods became violent and aggressive—everyone started to back away from him.

Shortly before the tragic accident Paul and John had experimented with collaborating on another form of creative expression. They had started work on a play called "Pilchard". Paul later described it as *". . . a sort of a precursor to Life Of Brian (the Monty Python movie) about a working class weirdo who is always upstairs praying. It was a down-market second coming. But we had to give it up because we couldn't actually work out how it went on, how you actually filled the pages.⁸⁹"*

August 1958

In early August The Quarry Men lost long time member Len Garry when he was diagnosed with Tubercular Meningitis and hospitalized. This effectively curtailed his time with the band. By the time he left the hospital The Quarry Men had moved on to new songs and new venues.

During the hiatus that followed the death of John's mother, Paul took an increasing leadership role in the group and its development.

Over the summer months of the school vacation period Paul had noticed a sign outside a house that advertised "Philips Recording Studio" and assumed it was in some way connected with the Phillips record company. Eventually he plucked up the courage to

---

* *John was actually 17 when he lost his mother.*

investigate further and discovered that the studio was an amateur one owned and operated by retired railway worker Percy Philips.

Paul inquired about the cost of cutting a demo. When he found out it would be less than £1 he booked a session for The Quarry Men without consulting the rest of the group.

On the appointed Saturday afternoon Paul arrived along with John Lennon, George Harrison, Colin Hanton and John Lowe. John was another school friend of Paul's from the Liverpool Institute who Paul had brought along because he *"could play like Jerry Lee Lewis.*[90]*"*

They were shown into the studio in the back room of Philips' house and did a quick sound check on the one and only microphone present. Despite the number of Lennon and McCartney tunes now available they chose to start with a familiar song, Buddy Holly's THAT'LL BE THE DAY.

When it came to deciding on a B-side, John was still feeling less than enthusiastic about things and didn't put forward any of his compositions. Thus it was that the first original "Beatles" tune ever recorded was not, as you'd expect a Lennon-McCartney tune but the McCartney-Harrison composition, IN SPITE OF ALL THE DANGER.

Their rendition of this regular Quarry Men stage number started to run long and Percy Philips started to wave frantically at them as the recording equipment neared its end.

The result was what must be the rarest Beatles recording in existence, an acetate single for which they paid a grand total of 17 shillings and 6 pence. The single was passed from person to person over the next few weeks and months eventually passing to John Lowe who held onto it for many years. Lowe eventually sold the acetate to Paul in the 1980s for an undisclosed sum.

Both John Lowe and Colin Hanton recall that the session was recorded direct onto the acetate as the cost to have a master tape made would have added an additional two shillings and sixpence to the cost.[91]

John, however, recalls that he returned to Philips' studio to obtain another pressing and was dismayed to discover that *"our stuff had been wiped off* (the master tape*) by some country and western singer.*[92]*"*

September 1958

Other than their foray into the amateur recording studio, The Quarry Men remained dormant for most of 1958. Paul and George would occasionally treat their classmates to impromptu performances of LONG TALL SALLY accompanied by school friend Dan Andrews. Their only other regular venue became the canteen at the Liverpool College of Art.

Paul and George would sneak over from the Institute next door, often eating their lunch sat with John and Stuart. Paul has said that he often learnt more from these lunch time sessions than he did at school, as the Art College crowd introduced him to a world of poetry, beatniks and the Bohemian lifestyle. At the time Paul and George seemed to resent John's "artsy" pretensions and his close relationship with Stuart. Almost as if Stuart was getting between them and John, diluting the strength they had developed as a trio. Given their young age, this subliminal anger would often surface in cutting remarks and put-downs.

Personal tensions aside, the major attraction in sneaking over to the college was the opportunity to play. John, Paul and George would hold impromptu jam sessions on the canteen stage or in Room 21 where the majority of John's classes were conducted. Here they would draw a small regular audience who listened to John run through his Buddy Holly numbers while Paul practiced his Little Richard impersonations or they would try their harmonies on an Everly Brothers tune. But, the ever-growing collection of original songs was kept hidden away from this early audience.

Among the audience was John's class mate, and future wife, Cynthia Powell. Cynthia had developed an interest in John and noticed a distinct change in him as he played. "*He looked positively beatific.*" His glasses were off and he relaxed as he sang . . . "*all that anger and malice in his face was gone.*" Cynthia Powell was transfixed by the John Lennon that emerged from the tough shell. She saw into the "*hurt helpless little boy underneath the rageful pose.*[93]"

December 1958

As the year drew to a close a new small coffee bar opened at 23 Slater Street close to the art college. Ex-plumber and wannabe club owner Allan Williams had been walking down the road and *"saw a For Lease sign above Owens Watch Repair Shop. The thought occurred to me that I could draw a lot of local people if I opened a coffee bar.*[94]*"*

Originally Williams wanted to call the club "The Samuari" but his friend Bill Coward had just read a book called "The Jacaranda Tree" and suggested a new name, "The Jacaranda Coffee Bar."

Today there is sign on the building at 23 Slater Street that says it was opened in 1957 (which is incorrect) and erroneously claims it as the place that "The Fab Four first played". The accompanying artwork depicts the Beatles—including Ringo—in Sgt Pepper costume. Although it's true that John, Paul, George and Ringo all played "The Jac", they never did as members of the same group.

The early clientele was mixed—attorneys, doctors, art students and musicians. The ground floor had a large glass window looking out on the street. There were small padded benches and coffee tables, a tiny kitchen and an outside toilet for the gents. A false trellis ceiling was installed from which fish nets and colored glass balls were hung. Steps lead down to the basement where the bands played. A small flight of stairs lead up to the Ladies room.

Allan Williams recalls that The Jac (as it soon became known locally) resembled *"a stale, tired waiting room in a railway station,*[95]*"* during the day but livened up in the evenings.

Coffee clubs were sprouting up all over Britain's cities and Liverpool was no exception. What set the Liverpool clubs apart was the fact that instead of having a jukebox they often featured live music from local bands.

The original house band at The Jacaranda was the All-Steel Caribbean Band with a line up comprising Allan Williams' friend "Lord Woodbine," and his group "Everett" "Otto" and "Slim".

Local photographer Cheniston K. Roland recalls that during the day the clients were businessmen, reporters and staff from local offices, but *"Night time was another story. Liverpool's youth became the customers. They were attracted to the club because Williams would let rock 'n' roll groups perform in the basement of the coffee bar. As a result The Jac became the meeting place for rock groups.*[96]"

According to one source[97] towards the end of 1958 some or all The Quarry Men played a few gigs under the name "The Rainbows." However no evidence has yet come to light to verify this. However the name "The Rainbows" occasionally surfaces in various stories about the early days of The Beatles in Liverpool so it can't be totally discounted. In at least one early interview Paul also mentioned that they once played under the name The Rainbows as *"we all had different colour shirts and we couldn't afford any others."*[98]

PART FOUR

"Rockin' The Casbah"—1959

January 1959

Although The Quarry Men hadn't performed in front of an audience for the majority of the previous six months, the Lennon and McCartney song writing team was still as productive as ever. Over the winter of 1958 and into early 1959 they penned numbers such as WHEN I'M 64 , LOVE OF THE LOVED , I'LL BE ON MY WAY, and A WORLD WITHOUT LOVE.*

Meanwhile twenty-four year old Brian Epstein was making another career move. The NEMS store at Charlotte Street had proved to be such a success that the family decided to open another branch closer to Liverpool city center at 12-14 Little Chapel.

Brian was asked to move across and manage this new flagship store. Using his theatrical contacts he even arranged for popular actor / singer Anthony Newly to open the store. Brian was highly impressed by the smartly dressed star and especially the way that he handled himself around the press and his fans. Newly's behavior would later become the model that Brian Epstein used for "*the way my artists (should) behave.*[99]"

---

* *Of these only "When I'm 64" was recorded by The Beatles themselves. However this early song-writing period supplied a stockpile of songs that other artists would take into the charts in later years. "Love Of The Loved" became a hit for Cilla Black in 1963, while another member of the Epstein stable, Billy J. Kramer recorded "I'll Be On My Way." "A World Without Love" became a #1 hit for Peter & Gordon whose career was launched and watched over by Paul.*

Early in January, possibly around the 7th, George's father, Harry Harrison, arranged for his son's band to play at a dance being held at the Social Club of the Merseyside Passenger Transport Executive, the local bus operators. Mr. Harrison was the chairman of the Social Club so arranging for his son's band to play wasn't too difficult. Perhaps a greater achievement was that he persuaded the manager of the local Pavilion cinema to "drop by" and watch The Quarry Men. The cinema manager was hoping to attract more teenagers to his movie house by having a local skiffle band play in the interval between the movies.

The dance was to be held at the Finch Lane bus depot. The evening started well with the group, albeit a bit rusty, performing their standard set without mishap. But over the break word was leaked to the boys that there were free drinks available for "the talent." The offer was too good to resist, especially for John who had taken to drinking even more following his mother's death.

The Quarry Men's second set was a complete shambles. The disgusted cinema manager sought out the group afterwards and openly criticized their performance and suggested that to get anywhere they would have to drastically improve their behavior and attitude. John's reaction was to tell the manager to "*piss off.*"[100]

The disgusted manager immediately withdrew his offer of a regular gig and stalked off. In the end he offered the regular cinema spot to The Darktown Skiffle Group whose line up now included Richard Starkey on drums. As the owner of one of the few full drum sets in Liverpool, Richie was in demand by nearly every skiffle group who needed a rhythm section. The "Eddie Clayton" group had started to drift apart and co-founder Eddie Mills was otherwise distracted by his impending marriage. Richie would now "non-committaly" sit in with any skiffle group that needed his services, even playing for three different outfits in one evening.

Meanwhile Quarry Men drummer Colin Hanton was also disgusted by the rest of the group's behavior. His complaints grew louder as they traveled home. It wasn't long before they were all involved in a full-scale argument on the bus. At the height of the argument Colin stormed off the bus, a stop earlier than he needed.

Taking his gear with him*, he never contacted the remaining members of The Quarry Men again.

The Quarry Men were now reduced to John Lennon, Paul McCartney and George Harrison.

It was as a trio for the first time that they honored an existing promise to play a gig at Woolton Village Hall on the 24th. But without the supporting sound produced by the drums and bass they realized that the group was going nowhere. The lack of a bass guitar was becoming a significant factor in stalling the progress of The Quarry Men away from being thought of as an amateur skiffle band towards being a rock 'n' roll group. A few months earlier Lou Walters, the bass player with Alan Caldwell's group had bought one of the new electric bass guitars on credit. Soon every rising group in Liverpool was exchanging their tea-chest basses for an electric version. Everyone, except the Quarry Men. John tried to persuade George to switch, but to no avail. His next tactic was to offer a place in the group to George's friend Arthur Kelley, on the proviso that he could find the £60 needed for a bass. This tactic didn't work either, so they were stuck as a group of three lead guitars.

Paul recalls that *"We'd show up for gigs, just the three of us with guitars. And the person who'd booked us would ask 'Where's the drums then?' To cover this we'd tell them "the rhythm's in the guitars.*[101]*"* But this excuse didn't work for long. With no rhythm or percussion, no regular gigs and no manager it was apparent that, after playing just twenty-five official gigs, for all effective purposes The Quarry Men were no more.

After just over two years John's "bit of fun" appeared to be over.

February 1959

Although probably at the lowest point of their career, the three principles kept playing together with the lunchtime jam sessions

---

* At the time of writing Colin Hanton is still in possession of the original Quarry Men drum kit.

at the art college. Paul and John kept working on new ideas and new songs. While George, keen to keep performing and playing, was soon "freelancing," as he later[102] termed this period.

George's first attempt to find experience outside of The Quarry Men was an audition for Alan Caldwell's new group "The Ravin' Texans." While impressed by George's ability and his rendition of Gene Vincent's *Wedding Bells*, they thought him too young and turned him down. Among the other hopefuls who failed to join the Ravin' Texans that day was Graham Bonnett who went on to achieve fame as a heavy metal front man with "Rainbow" in the 1980s.

Soon after, he was invited to join a new group called the "Les Stewart Quartet." Given the apparent lack of future for The Quarry Men, George was eager to gain more stage experience and play with a few other guys. He was also anxious to "*be in a band as opposed to having a job*.[103]" This and the prospect of a regular gig as the resident band at the Lowlands Club in Hymans Green, West Derby, where The Quarry Men had failed the audition the year before, meant George was soon on-board.

The Les Stewart Quartet comprised of Stewart on vocals, George and Ken Brown on guitar along with Geoff Skinner on drums. They became the regular Saturday night attraction at the Lowlands for the next seven months.

George had plenty of opportunities to split his time between Quartet rehearsals and lunch time jam sessions with John and Paul since he had stopped attending school. He was fast approaching his 16th birthday, on the 25th, but until then he was legally obliged to attend school. However legality was something that didn't concern him much. Due to his preoccupation with playing, George had sunk to the bottom of his class at The Liverpool Institute and failed all his subjects except art. To avoid problems at home he burnt his report card. He still left home in school uniform but never turned up for classes. Instead he spent his lunch money on weekday matinees at the local cinema and his spare time rehearsing with his guitar.

Not long after George joined his new band, he and his friends were shocked to learn of the death of one of their heroes in a plane crash. The "day the music died," February 3rd 1959, proved to be a pivotal event in the life of Paul McCartney. Buddy Holly's death inspired him to immediately compose I'LL FOLLOW THE SUN. And in the years to follow Paul became the leading champion of Buddy's legacy.

March 1959

On the 25th of March, Richard Starkey played his first gig as part of Al Caldwell's Ravin' Texans. It wasn't a full time position, just the first of a series of stand-in gigs as Richard still split his time with the Darktown Skiffle Group who were in the process of changing their image and name to a more rock 'n' roll friendly "The Cadillacs".[104]

He had meet Alan Caldwell earlier in the year at a talent search for the "6.5 Special" TV show held at the Liverpool Empire and was told that his group needed a drummer. Caldwell was fond of bestowing nicknames on most of his associates. Due to the number of rings Richard Starkey wore, the other members soon begin to call him "Ringo." The Ravin' Texans line-up was now settled at Alan Caldwell (vocals), Johnny Guitar (guitar), Ty Brown (guitar), Lu Walters (bass/vocals) and "Ringo" on drums.

April 1959

Now legally allowed to leave school, George applied for his first real job, as a window dresser at Blackler's department store in Liverpool, close to the new NEMS music store. The only vacancy the store personnel thought that the young Mr. Harrison was suitable for was that of apprentice electrician where the scruffy teddy boy would spend his time in the basement rather than in full view of the patrons. As it turned out George's rudimentary knowledge of electronics would be useful to the group before too long.

June 1959

Just down the road from The Lowlands Club where George played every Saturday stood a large Victorian house at 8 Hyman's Green, owned by the Best family, who had two teenage sons, Peter and Rory.

Both boys had lots of friends who were interested in rock 'n' roll. Their mother, Mona, suggested converting the seven-room cellar under the house into a meeting place for her sons' friends. It wasn't long before the idea progressed into plans for a proper club with a live band on weekends.

As it happened George's girlfriend, Ruth Morrison, was a family friend of the Best's. On hearing that this new club would need a band she suggested the group her boyfriend played with, "The Les Stewart Quartet." As Mona Best already knew Ken Brown she was easily convinced and they were "pencilled in" for the opening night scheduled in August.

Ken Brown recalled, *"At that time George Harrison and I were playing with The Les Stewart Quartet. The most we ever got was £2 for playing a wedding reception. Working Men's clubs never paid us more than 10 bob* (shillings). *It was George's girlfriend, Ruth Morrison, who told us that Mrs Best was opening the coffee bar. I went round to see Mrs. Best and we helped get the club ready. In return Mrs. Best said we could play at The Casbah when it finally opened."*[105]

Ken Brown was soon heavily involved in planning and decorating the club that had now been christened "The Casbah." In fact he became so involved that he started to miss rehearsals which upset Les Stewart.

The design of The Casbah, which got its name from a line in Mona Best's favorite movie, "Algiers," was to be a small intimate club with tables, fireplace, espresso machines and a bar which sold coffee, soda, hot dogs and crisps (chips). A jukebox was installed but no decision had yet been made as to where the live bands would perform. As a final touch Mona painted a Dragon on the ceiling. As well as the work on the cellars themselves, a living room upstairs was converted to a cloakroom and toilet facilities for both sexes were added.

August 1959

In mid August, about two weeks before the opening of The

Casbah, the ongoing argument between Les Stewart and Ken Brown over Ken's preoccupation with the club came to a head. *"Les and I got into an argument and Les said he wouldn't appear at the club. George and I walked out and I asked him if he knew anyone who could help. He said he had two mates and went off on a bus to fetch them. He returned in a couple of hours with his friends, Paul McCartney and John Lennon."*

Ken Brown has placed the argument on Casbah opening night, however Pete Best wrote that it happened two weeks previously. For other incidents to fall into some sort of logical order, Best's recollection is probably the most accurate.

Pete Best recalls that *"Ken came to Hymans Green with George in tow and told us they could make a foursome with a couple of friends.*[106]*"*

A few days later the four musicians, who had resurrected the name "Quarry Men" for their group, arrived at The Casbah for a tour of inspection. *"After five minutes gazing around the pre-opening chaos John made his plans,"* recalls Pete Best. *"A middle room, larger than most except the coffee bar itself, housed the jukebox. 'We'll play here' John decided. And that's the position that every band played from that day on.*[107]*"*

Mona Best, however, was not impressed by John's "prima donna" attitude and soon pressed the art college student into service as she handed him a paint brush. In hindsight this was probably not the best idea as the chronically shortsighted John was still averse to wearing his glasses in public. John, unable to read the labels on the paint can, applied a coat of gloss paint to the walls that left them still "tacky" by opening night.

The Casbah officially opened on Saturday the 29th of August. Membership was 2 shillings 6 pence a year or 1 shilling at the door. The doors opened at 7.30pm with the house band due on stage at 8.00pm. The house band was paid at a rate of £3 a night (15 shillings each). The line up for the new incarnation of The Quarry Men was John and George on lead, Paul and Ken on rhythm guitar with all amplification provided through Ken's cheap 10W amplifier wired together by apprentice electrician George. They performed "rent party" style all sat in a row, except for the person singing who would stand for their particular spot.

"*Among the songs we performed on opening night,*" says Brown, "*were 'LONG TALL SALLY', one of Paul's favorite pieces and 'THREE COOL CATS' which John sang, rolling his eyes. This made one chap laugh and John stopped playing and said 'belt oop lad' to him. John never took any nonsense from anyone in those days.*[108]"

Among the capacity crowd of 300 that opening night were the members of Alan Caldwell's band, including their new permanent drummer, "Ringo" Starkey. Caldwell had rechristened himself "Rory Storm" and his band now went under the name "Hurricanes." Also in the crowd was the Best's latest lodger, an accountancy student by the name of Neil Aspinall who had been in the same art and English classes as Paul McCartney at the Institute. Aspinall was destined to have a long association with The Beatles*.

The local West Derby paper reported on the opening of The Casbah, and while they concentrated on local boy Ken Brown and his efforts to help get the club ready, this article can arguably be counted as the first press notice for the embryonic Beatles.

> "*Kenneth Brown is also a member of a guitar group which entertains the club members on Saturday nights. The other members of the group, who call themselves The Quarry Men, travel from the south of the city to play.*[109]"

The day after the Casbah gig John decided to celebrate their new status as a "house band" by opening a hire-purchase agreement at Hessy's Music Store for the purchase of a Hofner Club 40 electric guitar. It wasn't long before George was also sporting a Hofner Club 40, but instead of buying his new guitar, George had traded his Hofner President for it with a member of The Swinging Blue Jeans.

---

*   *He became their driver and roadie shortly after their return from Hamburg at the end of 1960 and went on to become the longest tenured Beatles employee. At the time of writing he is still involved with Apple and was the executive producer of the Beatles Anthology project*

September 1959

The Quarry Men, for the first time in their short and turbulent history now had a residency. They played at The Casbah every Saturday night that month with gigs on the 10th, 19th and 26th.

After the gigs were over and the club emptied of paying customers, Pete Best started to mess around with the drum kits used by the other bands, including Ringo's. It has been suggested[110] that Pete even sat in with The Quarry Men on a few gigs around this time, but that seems unlikely. Pete didn't yet own his own drums and The Quarry Men certainly didn't have drum kit to call their own; plus Pete Best has never mentioned it.

October 1959

While "The Casbah" went from strength to strength, "The Cavern" was in financial trouble. The downturn in its fortunes started in late 1958 and by 12 months later the club was struggling to survive. A rival jazz club called 'The Mardi Gras Jazz Club" had opened in a better area of Liverpool and had started to attract the jazz devotees from The Cavern. The local skiffle bands were becoming less likely to play The Cavern due to owner Alan Sytner's policy of fining them for slipping rock numbers into their acts.

With the crowds diminishing and his alienation of the new breed of cheap home grown talent, the recently married Sytner moved to London and handed over the running of the club to his father. Dr. Sytner decided to try and attract people back by booking big name, and high cost, nationally recognized bands. The gamble failed and by mid-1959 The bands at The Cavern were playing to as few as 50 people. In stark contrast "The Iron Door" rock club located nearby was having to turn business away. Iron Door promoter and owner Sam Leach estimates he was pulling in as many as 2000 people for a Saturday night gig at that time.

Desperate to be rid of the burden the Sytner family sold the club to their accountant, Ray McFall, for the sum of £2,750. McFall appreciated all sorts of music and could see the success of nearby clubs like The Iron Door. As a result he had a more open policy and the local skiffle/rock bands started to trickle back. McFall also hired local personality, ex soldier and Liverpool Parks policeman, Pat 'Paddy" Delany, as a bouncer for his club, which was now officially known as "The Cavern"

The change in direction for the club was not immediately obvious as it "reopened" under new management on 3rd October with a performance from Acker Bilk And His Paramount Jazz Band. The same night The Quarry Men played, as usual, at The Casbah.

A week after the resurrection of The Cavern, and a day after John's 19th birthday on the 9th, The Quarry Men were to go through yet another line-up change. This gig was destined to be the last one that The Quarry Men played at The Casbah.

When the group arrived to set up for the evening gig, Mona Best was horrified to see that Ken Brown was suffering from a flu-like head cold (some reports say it was a twisted ankle). Whatever the cause he could hardly stand and was in no condition to play. Mrs. Best ushered him into a chair at the club door so he could collect the ticket money.

The gig itself went off without a hitch as John, Paul and George worked through their set as a trio. But when it came time to get paid, things turned ugly. Mona Best paid them each their 15 shilling fee, including Ken. Paul was incensed that Ken should be paid as he hadn't been on stage while they'd all been working. He felt that his fee should have been split between the three of them. Mona Best's response was that she paid the group a set fee of £3, and Ken was part of the group, and that by working the door (if that was the case) he had helped collect the money.

Paul's protests grew louder and John and George backed him up. The simple solution was that Ken shouldn't be part of the group. So from now on he wasn't—it was that simple. They had proved that evening they didn't need him—they would manage as a trio.

As a parting shot they swore that they would never play The

Casbah again. And they never did—well not as "The Quarry Men" anyway*.

Ken Brown's reaction was immediate and one that would have consequences for his departed colleagues within a year. Pete Best recalls; "*Down in the club I'd been having a tinker on the drums from time to time. After the '15 shilling incident' Ken said 'Why don't we form a group of our own Pete—Come on. You on drums.'—That was how The Blackjacks*** *were born.*"

"The Blackjacks" other members include Chas Newby (who would become The Beatles bass player for a short time in 1961) on lead guitar and Bill Barlow on bass. To get the group going Mona Best bought Pete a new drum kit from Blacklers department store, where George was still employed.

It wasn't long before Pete and Ken's group were alternating Saturday dates at The Casbah with Alan Caldwell's Ravin' Texans, now renamed "Rory Storm and his Hurricanes," with Ringo on drums. In fact a friendly competition evolved between the two as to who could pull the biggest crowd. The Blackjacks won, but only just.

"The Hurricanes" were fast becoming the top act on the Liverpool club circuit. Caldwell was first and foremost a performer and a promoter. He had already secured "The Ravin Texans" a one-off radio spot on Radio Luxemburg's "Skiffle Club," making them the first Liverpool group of this era to get any radio play. After changing the group's name, Caldwell legally changed his own name to Rory Storm and proceeded to live up to his new moniker. He would gyrate around the stage even more suggestively than Elvis. If the gig was held at a local swimming pool Storm would

---

* *After their return from Hamburg they once more became the house band at The Casbah, as the "The Beatles." Of course having Pete Best in the group by then was also an advantage to securing the residency. For a while, prior to the arrival of Brian Epstein, Mona Best even acted as the group's "manager and agent."*

** *The fact that Pete Best's first group had exactly the same name as that originally chosen by John Lennon for his first group is another of those strange "Beatles" coincidences*

sometimes climb the diving board, strip down to red swimming trunks and dive in as part of the act. The rest of the group were sometimes just as rowdy and boisterous. Ringo was even known to pitch drum sticks at hecklers in the audience. His drum solos got longer and the beat got heavier. The Hurricanes were fast developing into a power house of pure rock 'n' roll.

In stark contrast, now back to being a trio and without a regular gig, John, Paul and George returned to the talent show circuit almost immediately. The day after they quit The Casbah they turned up at Liverpool's Empire Theatre to audition for Carroll Levis's latest talent search. This time the ultimate prize was an appearance on Levis's TV show "Star Search."

As "The Quarry Men" had failed in their previous attempt, and worried that Levis might remember them, John decided to ditch the name in favor of a new one. So after three years, the name "Quarry Men" was resigned to history*. Instead Carroll Levis found himself auditioning "Johnny & The Moondogs." Levis was intrigued where the name came from and asked John what "moondogs" meant. John responded that it meant *"Red Indian who bangs tin cans together.*[111]" In fact the name was just typical John nonsense made up on the spur of the moment. John wanted something that stuck to the popular "lead singer & backing group" naming convention of the time.

Johnny & The Moondogs passed the audition and played in the two regional rounds at The Empire on the 18th and 25th October. The Liverpool round was won by "The Connaughts" featuring their old nemesis Nicky Cuff, the midget bass player. Johnny & The Moondogs finish third, just good enough to qualify for the next round to be held in nearby Manchester.

Rory Storm and The Hurricanes also tried out for The Carroll Levis show, finishing second in their round to Kingsize Taylor and The Dominoes.

---

* *The name would be resurrected years later by the surviving members of John's original band who perform as "The Quarrymen" at various Beatles related conventions and events*

To celebrate their success Johnny and his Moondogs headed to their latest haunt, "The Jacaranda" coffee bar. The coffee bar had become a regular spot for Paul and George. It was here that they often meet up with John and his college mate, Stuart Sutcliffe.

November 1959

November the 15th found John, Paul, and George on the train ride to Manchester for their first performance outside of the Merseyside area. They decided to concentrate on a set comprised of Buddy Holly songs, even practicing IT'S SO EASY on the train.

For some reason John was without a guitar at this point, according to Paul *"John must have sold or bust his guitar.*[112]" So the trio arrived with just Paul and George having instruments.

The competition was to be held at the Hippodrome on Hyde Road in Ardwick. A large baroque style theatre. The trio positioned themselves center stage. John was in the middle with his arms draped over Paul and George's shoulders. Due to Paul playing his guitar left-handed the two guitars pointed outwards giving a stylish effect. After a momentary silence they launched into the Buddy Holly songs THINK IT OVER and RAVE ON, sung by John and Paul. Although John and George sang together on WORDS OF LOVE, another Holly song, it was already becoming obvious that what set Johnny & The Moondogs apart from the other groups was the vocal interplay between Lennon and McCartney.

After their set John, Paul and George hung around backstage until they had to rush to leave and catch the last train back to Liverpool. Their baggage now included three guitars as John appeared to have "acquired" one somewhere backstage[113].

Unfortunately for "The Moondogs" the competition was to be decided on a "clapometer" which measured the volume of the audience response when each act was brought back on stage at the end of the show. When it came time for Johnny & The Moondogs to receive their applause, they were sat on the train home, being unable to afford a hotel room.

None of the other Liverpool bands in attendance, including Rory Storm & The Hurricanes fared any better. The winners of the "Star Search" were Manchester locals "Ricky & Dane." "Ricky & Dane" were in fact Allen Clarke and Graham Nash—later of The Hollies (named for Buddy Holly), Graham Nash went on to even greater stardom in Crosby, Stills and Nash . Also on the bill that night were Billy Fury, who would cross paths with John, Paul and George again within the year, and Freddie Garrity who would later find fame as lead singer of Freddie & The Dreamers.

Following their return to Liverpool, George decided to once again upgrade his guitar, maybe to keep pace with the new one that John had "obtained" in Manchester. On November 20th he opened a hire-purchase account at Hessy's and put down his first payment on a new Futurama 5 electric guitar.

A few days after the Manchester gig the John Moore's art exhibition opened at The Walker Art Gallery, William Brown St in Liverpool. It featured a piece by John's friend Stuart Sutcliffe. In fact Stuart had been working on the abstract expressionist piece for months. It was designed to be a huge canvas, 8 feet by eight feet, divided into two sections. Once it was completed Rod Murray and Stuart delivered the first section to the gallery then headed for the pub before going back to Percy Street to collect the second section. Here they were confronted by the landlady who had found a piece of her antique furniture smoldering in the fireplace. She ordered the boys out within the hour.

Rod and Stuart located a new flat at 3 Gambier Terrace, where they were soon joined by a new tenant, John Lennon. However during the rush to move, the second section of Stuart's painting was totally forgotten and it never made it to the show at The Walker. Unaware that it was only one-half of a much bigger piece, the exhibition committee selected Stuart's "Summer Painting" for show. It was the only student piece selected.

It was an honor to be selected, and to add to Stuart's success, art patron John Moore, the exhibition's benefactor, bought his painting for 50 Guineas (£65).

John's immediate response to his friend's windfall was to suggest that Stuart use it to buy a much needed bass for his group and become a member.

John's girlfriend, Cynthia, recalls that the "official" offer for Stuart to join "The Moondogs" was made at the Gambier Terrace flat. Paul recalls that the invitation was made on Friday evening at The Casbah, where they still hung out, even if they were no longer playing there.

Wherever the offer was made the underlying reason was that no-one else wanted to play the bass, but they all recognized that without a regular drummer they needed some rhythm behind the guitars. Paul recalls John persuading Stuart, "*Get a bass man, because then you could be in the band. And it's not hard, bass, you don't have to know lots of chords and stuff.* [114]"

Several of Stuart's friends expressed dismay at him joining John's group. Even Bill Harry, despite his enthusiasm for rock 'n' roll in general and John's group in particular, expressed concerns. Many felt that Stuart was such a talented artist that he should have focused on his natural talents. But, rock 'n' roll was fun for Stuart, a way to escape and relax.

December 1959

As the year closed John turned his creative talents to writing by producing a special version of Cinderella for the College Of Art's Christmas pantomime. The "panto" was performed in the basement canteen of the college with John playing one of the Ugly Sisters[**] while Stuart played the Fairy Snow.

1959 had been a year of change for John, Paul and George. They had started out with no real musical direction. In fact they hadn't even really had a group. Yet, by the year end they'd reformed, played and lost their first residency, had some success in national competition and found that elusive bass player. All they needed now was a drummer and a name.

[**] *John's costume from this art college production was auctioned by Christies in 1988*

PART FIVE

"Moondogs to Beatles"—1960

January 1960

Johnny & The Moondogs started off what was to be their pivotal year in low key style with a gig at the Cassanova Club on the 10th. Still a trio, they played to a small but enthusiastic crowd at the rock 'n' roll club which was located above the Temple Restaurant in Dale Street Liverpool. This would be their last gig as a trio.

A week later Stuart Sutcliffe officially joined the group. It could have been John's powers of persuasion or just the desire to get involved in the other side of John's life, but whatever the reason on 21st January Stuart found himself outside Hessy's music store. It wasn't long before he emerged with a large Hofner 333 bass. Legend has it that Stuart spent the £65 pounds from the art sale on this bass and that it was a light wood "blonde" model. A recently discovered receipt in Hessy's archives shows that, like the rest of the group, he signed a hire-purchase agreement and placed a £15 deposit with the rest of his weekly payments bringing the total cost of the guitar to £59. It also says that the Hofner was a "brunette" finish.

After joining the band Stuart threw all his energy and enthusiasm into playing and as a result his art started to suffer, much to the dismay of his friends and teachers. He hardly saw any of his old friends any more, spending all his time with John. Several put it down to John being a bad influence when in fact it was Stuart who had a greater influence on John and the rest of the band.

During his time with the band Stuart was often ridiculed by them for his playing abilities. However, as George put it, "*It was better to have a bass player who couldn't play than not to have a bass player at all.*"[115] John and Paul would generally make fun of him on stage. John could be "cruelly sarcastic" while he received "general abuse from the band who didn't take him seriously.' John—"*We'd tell Stuart he couldn't sit with us, or eat with us. We'd tell him to go away and he did.*"[116]

Stuart's mother Millie recalled that "*When Stuart asked John to teach him how to play the bass, John replied 'it takes me all the time to teach myself. I hardly know two chords. I'm guessing as I go.' So he refused to help Stuart.*"[117]

In fact John had asked Dave May, bass player with local group The Silhouettes, to teach Stuart a few basics starting with the bass part for Eddie Cochran's COME ON EVERYBODY. But progress was slow and painful as Stuarts fingers started to harden and callous. The damage to his fingers also started to cause concern among his Art College tutors.

Despite the bickering and the apparent lack of support, John and Stuart were becoming even more inseparable as friends. The two were now almost soul mates; almost perfect reflections of each other's desires. For Stuart was the bohemian artist that John aspired to be, while John represented the streetwise character that Stuart sometimes wished he could be.

February 1960

A lower key event, but one that was to have significance a few years later was the decision by Ray McFall, owner of The Cavern, to replace the regular skiffle sessions with a lunchtime rock 'n' roll session. These new spots were to be held every Wednesday through Friday and were soon drawing the largest crowds to The Cavern, easily surpassing the attendance for the traditional evening Jazz sessions.

It would be a few years later, at one of these Cavern lunchtime sessions, that Brian Epstein would see The Beatles in action for the first time.

March 1960

In early March, London based promoter Larry Parnes promoted a show for the American rock 'n' rollers Eddie Cochran and Gene Vincent at The Liverpool Empire. Jacaranda owner Allan Williams attended. After seeing the reaction of the fans, and being quick to realize an opportunity when it presented itself, Williams approached Parnes and introduced himself with the idea of holding a bigger concert in Liverpool headlined by Parnes' acts with support from a number of local bands. Parnes was intrigued by the proposition and promised to contact Williams later in the year.

Parnes was the most successful pop impresario of the late 1950s and early 1960s in Britain (until eclipsed by Brian Epstien). He was known as "Mr. Parnes, Shilling & Pence" because of his alleged reluctance to pay his artists. Brian Epstein also met Larry Parnes backstage at the same event where he was introduced as a *"local record store manager, interested in the pop business.*[118]*"*

Also in the audience that day were Paul, George, John and his girlfriend Cynthia, along with Stuart and his girlfriend Veronica Johnson. According to Veronica[119], John spent most of the evening complaining, in an overwhelming example of prescient irony, that he couldn't hear the music over the screaming of the female fans.

George was such a fan of Cochran's that he used some of his newly acquired wages to travel to another couple of Cochran gigs in nearby towns so he could watch the guitarist at work and learn his techniques from afar.

Since he had joined the group Stuart had been helping John in the search for a new name. They played around with a number of combinations that followed the tradition of "lead singer & backing group" formula. As both John and Paul had been influenced by Buddy Holly, they started to look for a similar themed name to his group "The Crickets."

Stuart appears to have come up with the name Beetles. Employing his talent for word play John decided to turn the second "e" into an "a" to make the name a pun on the word "beat"—The Beatles.

John later recalled *"I was looking for a name like Crickets that meant two things. Then from Crickets I eventually got to Beetles. I changed the 'beet' part to 'beat' and then it meant two things. When you said it people thought of crawly things, and when you read it, it said beat music."*[120]

Over the years numerous stories have developed over the naming of The Beatles. John himself was the first to spin a tale when a few years later (in 1961) he wrote an article for the first issue of the *Mersey Beat* newspaper on "Being a short Diversion on the Dubious Origins of The Beatles." In this humorous and irreverent article he revealed that *"It came in a vision—a man appeared on a flaming pie and said unto them 'From this day on you are Beatles with an A.' Thank you, Mister Man, they said, thanking him."*[121]

One story that seems to have been repeated over the years is that John, and possibly Stuart, were influenced by a scene in the 1953 Marlon Brando movie "The Wild Ones" when biker Lee Marvin utters a line in which he appears to call a motorcycle gang "The Beetles." While the movie was influential with a lot of the early American rockers it is highly unlikely to have had any impact on John Lennon by 1960. "The Wild Ones" was banned in the UK for many years and was not seen in the British cinema until 1968. This story is definitely one that grew and was perpetuated after-the-fact. The Beatles themselves have, to some extent, perpetuated this myth by including the relevant movie clip as the opening sequence on the Anthology video series.

Another popular story is that it was promoter Larry Parnes who suggested to the group that "they get a better name for themselves, something like Buddy Holly's Crickets." But as they were already calling themselves "The Silver Beetles" when Parnes first met them later in the year—this is unlikely.

Despite all the wonderful stories about how this, the most famous of group names, came into existence, the truth is that John Lennon was still as much a Buddy Holly fan as he had been two years early when he wrote a fan letter to the drummer of Buddy's backing group, The Crickets.

The name Beatles was a simple homage. Ironically The Crickets themselves had considered "Beetles" during their search for a group name. "(We got) *an encyclopedia and somehow got started on insects. There was a whole page of bugs. We thought about grasshoppers and quickly passed that one over. And we did consider the name Beetles but (someone) said 'that's just a bug you step on' so we immediately dropped that.*"[122]

Despite having come up with a name, John and Stuart weren't comfortable enough with it to know how it would be perceived by the public. So the newly named group played its next gig, in mid March, as the tentatively titled "Beatals," pronounced as "Beat-alls."

With the freshly coined name in mind Stuart tried his hand at getting the group some engagements. In a draft of a letter dated 27th March 1960[123], he wrote:

> "*I would like to draw your attention to a band, to the 'Beatals'. This is a promising group of young musicians who play music for all tastes, preferably rock and roll.*" It is signed "*Stu Sutcliffe (Manager)*"

April 1960

In early April of 1960, the group had taken to rehearsing at the McCartney home. One such session was captured on a home tape recorder and provides the only permanent record of Stuart Sutcliffe's time with the group. The three tracks captured that day were Ray Charles's HALLELUJAH, I LOVE HER SO; an early Lennon-McCartney song YOU'LL BE MINE and an instrumental by Paul entitled CAYENNE.

Meanwhile plans for the big Liverpool concert were progressing until Allan Williams learnt the devastating news that Eddie Cochran and Gene Vincent had been involved in a car accident on the 17th of April in the West of England returning from a Parne's concert in Bristol. Cochran had been killed and Vincent was seriously injured.

With the Liverpool Institute and Art College on spring break,

Paul and John decided to undertake a road trip. They eventually wound up in the Berkshire town of Caversham where Paul's cousin Elizabeth and her ex-Redcoat husband, Mike Robbins, now operated a pub called The Fox & Hounds.

The two teenagers soon pitched in helping behind the bar and cleaning tables. Mike suggested that in the evenings they might like to play a few songs for the customers. So for two nights in the tap room of a rural English pub, John Lennon and Paul McCartney played songs perched on barstools strumming their acoustic guitars. They billed themselves as "The Nerk Twins" a name suggested by Mike Robbins.

On the return from his road trip John left his Aunt's house to move in with Stuart Sutcliffe and fellow art student Rod Murray at a flat in 3 Gambier Terrace about 100 yards from the College.

The group often rehearsed at the flat and Bill Harry (later founder and editor of the Mersey Beat newspaper and author of several Beatles books) was a regular visitor. Also a regular overnight visitor was John's girlfriend Cynthia who used to cover her absences from home by telling her mother that she was staying with her good friend Phyllis McKenzie.

The Jacaranda had now become the regular haunt for all the art college students. And given Allan William's interest in the burgeoning rock scene, he had also encouraged as many of the local bands to play there as well. John, Stuart, Paul and George were now regulars at the coffee bar. In fact during this time Alan Williams asked Stuart to paint some murals in the bar. Stuart did and Rod Murray helped—although years later Alan Williams claimed it was Stuart and John. Although he was a big admirer of Stuart's artistic skill and general bohemian attitude, Williams made several disparaging remarks about the group's musical talent and the fact that they weren't getting anywhere, to which John challenged *"well why don't you do something for us."*

Allan Williams agreed to manage the group, *"(He)was a great bloke, a good motivator, perfect for us at the time.[124]"* One of the first things he did as manger was to suggest that they go for a more pop type of name. He suggested "Long John & The Silver Beetles." His suggestion was greeted with howls of derisive laughter, but a compromise was reached and the group would now perform under the name "The Silver Beetles."

May 1960

As the Silver Beetles struggled, Richard Starkey was facing the decision as to whether he should become a full-time professional musician. Rory Storm & The Hurricanes had been booked for a full summer season at Butlins holiday camp in Pwllheli, Wales for £25 a week headlining at the Rock & Calypso Ballroom. The lengthy and lucrative summer time gig had been arranged through Rory Storm's sister Iris Caldwell who was a Redcoat at the camp. A summer job at Butlins was also known to be a good starting point for the UK's burgeoning pop stars. Cliff Richard and Joe Brown would get their starts there. Another attraction was that the holiday company had its own record label.

"Ringo" was reluctant to give up his day job at Hunts. His parents, Elsie and Harry, wanted him to complete his apprenticeship and "get a trade." But, Richie was eventually persuaded by the prospect of extra money and the fact that Rory had promised to introduce a new "Starr Time" spotlight part for his drummer. It wasn't long before Richard Starkey was going under the name "Ringo Starr." His mind was made up—he resigned from Hunts and would spend the summer of 1960 at Butlins. *"As good as a holiday and you get paid for it."*[125]

Before leaving for North Wales, The Hurricanes were scheduled to play for Allan Williams at the "Larry Parnes Concert."

Despite the tragic death of Eddie Cochran, his friend Gene Vincent, still recovering from his injuries of broken ribs and collar bone, discharged himself from hospital to honor the date he had agreed to play in Liverpool.

"The Greatest Show Ever To Be Staged" was promoted under the banner of "Jacaranda Enterprises, by arrangement with Larry Parnes" and was scheduled to last 3 hours on the 3rd May 1960 and would be held at the 6,000 seat sports arena near Prince's Docks.

The show was opened by the struggling Gene Vincent who paid tribute to his lost friend with an emotional rendition of SOMEWHERE OVER THE RAINBOW. Although still too injured to perform his usual set and using the microphone stand for support, Vincent introduced the other acts from the Parnes stable. In the absence of the late Eddie Cochran the task of headlining the concert fell to American blues singer Davy Jones (The following year,1961, The Beatles played a couple of gigs as his backing group). Jones was followed by several of Parnes' "b-string" acts. It's obvious from the line up that Parnes was still far from convinced about the potential of Williams' "Greatest Show Ever." Nero & His Gladiators, Lance Fortune, Dean Webb, The Viscounts, Julian X, Colin Green & The Beat Boys were hardly the cream of Parnes "stable of the stars" and probably not any more skilled, although undoubtedly better polished, than the local groups that Allan Williams supplied.

The local boys followed after the interval. The Liverpool line up assembled by Williams included Rory Storm & The Hurricanes with Ringo on drums**, Cass & The Cassanovas, Gerry & The Pacemakers, Mal Perry, and The Connaughts. Unfortunately a tape recording made of this unique concert was erased shortly afterwards.

Amongst the crowd sat Paul, John, George and Stuart. Allan Williams was still far from convinced of their potential and had not included them.

After the show Parnes was so impressed by the local bands that he asked Allan Williams to arrange a series of auditions so Parnes could find backing bands for some of his solo acts during their upcoming summer tours. Stuart Sutcliffe was angry at The Silver Beetles' exclusion from the concert that had been arranged and promoted by their "manager". He approached Alan Williams for an explanation. As a "peace offering" to Stuart, Williams offered to make sure the Silver Beetles were short-listed for the Parnes auditions.

** *A photograph taken at this concert is the earliest known picture of Ringo playing on stage.*

Within a couple of days of making his promise, Allan Williams solved The Silver Beetles other outstanding problem—their lack of a drummer. On the 5th of May he introduced them to Tommy Moore. Since agreeing to do "something" for Stuart's group, as he saw them, Williams had been asking around if anyone knew a drummer and Brian Casser, of Cass & The Cassonovas, suggested Tommy Moore. Williams made a trip to Garston Bottle Works where Moore drove a forklift for a living. He found the drummer and offered him the job, which Tommy accepted. Tommy and John disliked each other from almost the moment they meet. John took to continuously throwing caustic remarks at the drummer, particularly about his "advanced" age. Tommy was 26 and more of a jazz fan than a rocker.

With an experienced drummer now in the line-up, Williams thought he had a real group and offered them a regular spot as back-up band at The Jacaranda. They could play a regular spot when Lord Woodbine and his friends were on a break.

Events started to move quickly as the following day, 6th May, a letter arrived at The Jacaranda from Mark Forster, assistant to Larry Parnes. The letter confirmed Parnes' request for a series of auditions and added more detail.

> "... *Duffy Power will be touring Scotland from June 2nd to June 11th inclusive* ... *And Johnny Gentle will be touring Scotland from June 16th to June 25th. For those two periods, as agreed, we are willing to pay your groups £120 plus the fares from Liverpool. Should you agree to these suggestions we will arrange for Duffy and Johnny, who incidentally is a Liverpool boy, to travel up to Liverpool to rehearse with your groups towards the end of May ...*
>
> *We will (also) make arrangements for Mr Parnes to come and audition your groups to select the most suitable. He will also bring Billy Fury as Billy will want one of these four groups for his own personal use. Incidentally the idea of Billy wanting a group from his home town will provide several interesting press stories and publicity tie-ups.*"[126]

The four groups finally chosen, as per Parnes' letter, were Gerry & The Pacemakers, Cass & The Cassanovas, Cliff Roberts & The Rockers, Derry & The Seniors. Not forgetting his promise to Stuart, Allan Willams added The Silver Beetles to the list even though it pushed the number of bands above the amount specified by Parnes.

The letter from Parnes' office turned out to be inaccurate in terms of tour dates as Johnny Gentle's tour of Scotland was in fact scheduled for later in May. As a result the audition was hastily arranged for the 10th.

The audition was held at The Wyvern Social Club at 108 Seel Street. The club had recently been leased by Williams who had plans to turn it into a top night club.(Williams eventually opened The Blue Angel club at this location in 1961) For the moment it provided more room than the Jacaranda and could easily accommodate the five hopeful groups and the Parnes entourage.

The audition session was the chance for the Liverpool boys to get the "big break" and hook up with the most successful manager and promoter in the UK at the time. The presence of a couple of local Liverpool boys who had already "made it", Billy Fury• and Johnny Gentle gave the "event" an even greater mystique for the struggling groups. It attracted members of several groups that had not been selected, notably Rory Storm, who turned up to see and be seen, and maybe snatch a few minutes with the "big boys" from London. A couple of attendees also brought cameras along to record the session.

As the auditions started the only noticeable absentee was The Silver Beetles new drummer Tommy Moore. No real explanation has been given for his tardiness. Some sources have suggested that

---

• *Legend has it that Fury literally broke into show-business. Encouraged by his friend, and future TV comedian, Jimmy Tarbuck, unemployed tug boat hand Ronnie Wycherly broke into the dressing room at one of Parnes' shows in nearby Birkenhead. He performed a song he'd written to Parnes and star act Marty Wilde. Parnes was impressed enough to put the cheeky teenager on stage in the second half. The girls in the audience swooned over his looks. Parnes signed him that evening and changed his name to "Billy Fury".*

Moore was a "rent-a-drummer" hired specifically for the audition and he was off collecting his drum set from a previous engagement. Other sources suggest he was having a problem getting away from the bottle factory where he worked.

The audition was kicked off with Cass & The Cassanovas, followed by Derry & The Seniors and then Gerry & The Pacemekers. After the first three groups Parnes called for a break to compare notes. During the break John nervously approached Billy Fury to ask for an autograph. A photograph taken at the time has star Billy Fury center frame, but John can just be seen on the edge holding out a piece of paper for Fury to sign, the paper is covered with John's now familiar doodles. For all his bohemian pretensions at this stage, John was still the star-struck nineteen year-old rock 'n' roll fan.

The break over, it was the turn of the final two groups to audition. Cliff Roberts and The Rockers lead off to be followed by The Silver Beetles. Allan Williams had moved "his boys" to last place in the hope that this would give Tommy Moore time to arrive. As they took up position there was still no sign of Moore.

All the groups had performed in their flashy stage costumes, but The Silver Beetles were clad in basic outfits of black jeans, black shirts and matching tennis shoes. Another indication of their lack of local success and money to date was the fact that they obviously borrowed equipment from other groups. Photos taken that day clearly show them using amps labeled with the name of another local group "The Pressmen."

At the last minute Johnny Hutchinson, the drummer from Cass & The Cassanovas, agreed to provide the rhythm section. Photos taken as they went through their first few numbers show Hutchinson looking incredibly bored and a little embarrassed to be sat behind these "amateur schoolboys." These photos have led some researchers[127] to conclude that Hutchinson was the groups' permanent drummer at this stage**. The same photographs show

---

** It has been suggested that in 1962 several people recommended Johnny Hutchinson to Brian Epstein as first choice to replace Pete Best rather than Ringo.

John and Paul are out front giving it all they've got with John adopting a Gene Vincent like stance. George is slightly off to one side concentrating on his guitar playing. Stuart is stood far to John's right turned sideways on to the watching impresario.

Paul recalls that Stuart adopted this sideways stance at the request of the rest of the group, *"We'd ask Stuart to turn away slightly in case people noticed he wasn't quite keeping up. He'd be in A and we'd be in A Flat, and we didn't want anyone to notice.*[128]*"*

Tommy Moore eventually arrived when The Silver Beetles were a couple of numbers into the set and took his place behind the drums. Judging from the photographs taken at this point the number they sang was slower with John and Paul harmonizing close around a single mike. Stuart had turned his back to the audience as he was struggling with the bass part. This photo is probably the cause of the popular misconception that Stuart always played with his back to the audience.

After the audition was over Larry Parnes delivered his verdict, Cass & The Cassanovas would back Billy Fury on his upcoming tour.

According to Allan Williams, Billy Fury was in favor of having The Silver Beetles but was overruled by Parnes. Williams says that Parnes "saw through" Stuart's back-to-the-audience routine and asked them to play another number without Stuart. John apparently refused, stating that they played with Stuart or not at all. Parnes has always refuted this account saying that his problem with the group was Tommy Moore's late arrival and his age. This is a position that he has strongly defended over the years, even threatening to sue Paul in 1982 after Paul made some adverse comments about the audition on the Desert Island Discs radio show.

Others at the audition were less than impressed by The Silver Beetles. Howard Casey the lead singer of Derry & The Seniors said later, *"I can't remember them* (being at the audition) *or what they played.*[129]*"*

Having failed to secure the Billy Fury tour gig, The Silver Beetles returned to the local scene. On May 14th they played an unadvertised gig at the Lathom Hall, Lathom Ave, in Liverpool's

Seaforth district as "The Silver Beats" playing during the interval as an audition for local promoter Brian Kelly.

Kelly was one of several Liverpool promoters who used the practice of "auditioning" groups by having them play a set during a "gap" in a live show, thereby getting their services for free. "The Silver Beats" auditioned in the interval between performances from "Kingsize Taylor & The Dominoes", "Cliff Roberts & The Rockers," and "The Deltones". Kelly booked the band for a paid gig on the 21st.

Drummer Cliff Roberts recalled The Silver Beats as *"a scruffy bunch whose drummer hadn't brought his kit."* They asked to borrow Robert's kit but he refused to lend it to Tommy Moore so he sat in with the Silver Beats and played six numbers with them, *"four rock-n-roll standards that all the groups played and two originals they had to teach me.*[130]*"*

In the audience that night was Pete Best. The Best's lodger Neil Aspinall later claimed that it was at this gig that *"two trouble makers followed Stu Sutcliffe into the dressing room muttering things like 'get your hair cut girl'. John and Pete (Best) went after them and a fight broke out and John broke his finger.*[131]*"* Many writers say this was the fight where Stuart received the head injury that would prove fatal in the years to come. Stuart Sutcliffe's mother has claimed that Stuart received his fabled head injury after falling down a flight of stairs in Hamburg. She has also said that it happened after a gig in January 1961 and John broke his wrist helping Stuart. Pete Best recalls John's broken finger but no injury to Stuart while other sources say Pete helped John rescue Stuart from the beating. Stuart's sister also dates this fight as 30th January 1961 at the Lathom Hall, and agrees the head injury occurred in Hamburg but gives a totally different cause[132].

Larry Parnes hadn't forgotten The Silver Beetles. On the 18th he contacted Allan Williams and offered them the slot as backing group for the Johnny Gentle tour of Scotland due to start on the 20th.

This meant that "the boys" had to arrange things quickly. It was easy for John and Stuart to free up time as they were hardly going to any classes at Art College anymore. Paul persuaded his father that the tour would be good experience before he went back to school to further his studies. George solved the problem by quitting his job at Blackers. Tommy Moore had a harder job freeing up his schedule and had to use some of his vacation time, much to the disgust of his girlfriend.

The next day they were on the train to Scotland. The group's name had once again been the topic of discussion as various people in the Parnes camp didn't like the connotations of the word "beetles." One of the first names proposed was "Long John Silver & The Pieces of Eight,[133]" but a compromise was reached and the group stayed as "The Silver Beatles." But the boys adopted stage names;

Stuart went under the name "Stuart De Stael" named for his favorite painter.

George adopted the name "Carl Harrison" in honor of guitar hero Carl Perkins.

Paul adopted the name Paul Ramone. The longest lived of The Beatles pseudonyms, Paul used the name again in 1969, when he assisted The Steve Miller Band on *"My Dark Hour."* It's also been suggested that the quintessential punk band The Ramones named themselves after Paul's alter-ego.

There is some dispute as to whether John adopted the stage name "Long John" for the tour. The rest of the group insists that John used the name, although he always denied it.

He was so insistent that years later he sent the authors of The Beatles: Illustrated Record clippings from the time to prove his point. Unfortunately the clippings actually related to a gig in Neston immediately after the group's return from Scotland and did nothing to clarify the issue.

Tommy Moore refused to join in with the youthful role playing.

Johnny Gentle, also originating from Liverpool and whose real name was John Askew and wasn't much older than the Beatles at 22, was less than impressed by the ensemble that got off the train in Alloa. *"When I first saw them, I wondered what on earth Parnes had sent me.*[134]" However 30 minutes of rehearsal were enough to convince Gentle that his backing group was something special.

But not everyone was impressed. The Parnes tour manager, Duncan McKinnon, an elderly chicken farmer from Dumfries, immediately complained to Parnes on the phone about the "scruffy" look of The Silver Beetles and wanted them sacked. Gentle intervened and arranged for them to have a more presentable look by donating a selection of black shirts to wear on stage.

On the 20th May 1960 The Silver Beetles made their professional debut at Alloa Town Hall, Scotland. Billed as "Johnny Gentle & The Silver Beetles" they topped the bill supported by local ballad singer Bobby Rankins and The Alex Harvey Band. Alex Harvey eventually became a close friend of The Beatles during their Hamburg days and went on to be a successful rocker in his own right before his untimely death in the seventies.

The running order that night established the pattern for the rest of the tour. The standard show routine was for The Silver Beetles to come on first and do six numbers. Johnny Gentle would then come on and do his spot. After he left the stage the boys would conclude the show with another six number set. Each set comprised mainly of rock and roll numbers such as BLUE SUEDE SHOES, ROCK 'N' ROLL MUSIC and LONG TALL SALLY.

The following night "Johnny Gentle & The Silver Beetles" traveled on to a gig at Northern Meeting Ballroom, Church Street, Inverness, Scotland. The venue was split into two halls. Performing in the main hall on the ground floor was Lindsay Ross and his Dance Band. While The Silver Beetles were consigned to the small upstairs hall sharing a bill with Ronnie Watt and the Chekkers Rock Dance Band. At the Inverness gig Paul was asked for his autograph for the first time and wrote home excitedly to his father that he "*Signed for them too, three times!*"[135]

That same evening "The Silver Beats" were advertised as the headline act at Lathom Town Hall in Liverpool by Brian Kelly, who was unaware they were in Scotland. Kelly was upset by the lack of notice from the group that he made sure that they didn't get any more gigs during the rest of 1960. Kelly eventually forgave The Beatles this oversight as he booked them again in 1961, following their return from Hamburg.

Meanwhile, unaware that they'd closed off one potential avenue of employment back in Liverpool, The Silver Beetles were on the road to Fraserborough in Aberdeen for a gig at Dalrymple Hall on the 23rd.

On the way to this gig Johnny Gentle insisted on driving the tour bus instead of the regular driver, Gerry Scott, and promptly crashed into the back of a stationary Ford Popular occupied by two old ladies. The only casualty was Tommy Moore who suffered a chipped tooth from a flying guitar case. (Some accounts say he lost two front teeth, and suffered a concussion). Moore was anesthetized while his cut face and lips were stitched up. The promoter at Dalrymple Hall was insistent on the number of musicians he'd booked performing so the band dragged the semi-conscious Moore out of his hospital bed, still groggy from the effects of the pain killers, to play the gig.

On the 25th "Johnny Gentle & The Silver Beetles" played a gig at St. Thomas Hall, Deith. But perhaps of greater significance to the future career of the group was that back in Liverpool The Cavern held its first evening rock 'n' roll session featuring Cass & The Cassanova's and Rory Storm & The Hurricanes, featuring Ringo Starr, playing their last local gig before their Butlins engagement.

Cavern owner Ray McFall's decision was based on pure business reasoning rather than any sense of remarkable foresight. "*A dozen or more suburban halls on the outskirts were flourishing . . . I decided to make The Cavern Liverpool's first city-center Rock-n-Roll club. At the time I couldn't have dreamed of the destiny that lay ahead . . . To me the introduction of rock'n'roll merely meant drawing in a separate and bigger crowd.*"

The following night The Cavern's future stars played a gig at Forres Town Hall, Scotland. The Silver Beetles didn't receive any billing. The gig was advertised locally as "Johnny Gentle and his Group". They were also advertised as a "dance band" with the dance being held from 9.00pm to 1.00am with an entrance fee of 5 shillings. The other act on the bill was Rikki Barnes and his all Stars. The meager wages they were being paid had all but run out and didn't cover their expenses. "The Silver Beetles" had run out of money. In fact they were so short of cash that they slipped out of the Royal Hotel in Forres the following morning without paying their bill.

George recalled that "*We were like orphans (on that tour) with holes in our shoes and our trousers were a mess. While the Parnes fellow, Johnny Gentle, had a posh suit and stuff. I remember trying to play with no amplifiers, we were crummy, we were an embarrassment.*[136]"

Although the tour was a disaster financially and morally, it did consolidate their standing professionally. By this half-way mark they were starting to outshine the headlining star who they were meant to be backing. Gentle was impressed enough to suggest to Larry Parnes that he sign them. Parnes, at that time, only managed solo acts and declined. "*Johnny used to phone me virtually every night and say 'come up to Scotland and see the boys. I've given them a spot in my act and they are doing better than I am.'*[137]"

The tour was completed with gigs at the Royal Ballroom, Leopold St, Nairne, on the 27th at the Rescue Hall, Peterhead, Aberdeen on the 28th.

During the tour Gentle had been working on a song called "I've Just Fallen For Someone" and was helped out by John. The song was eventually recorded by Gentle under his later stage name of Darren Young.

During the tour George got friendly with Johnny Gentle and Gentle presented George with an old stage shirt once worn by Eddie Cochran. George later recalled "*That tour was our first faint hope of actually making it someday.*[138]"

By the 29th The Silver Beetles were on the train back to Liverpool while Johnny Gentle remained in Scotland. Paul, John, George and Stuart were under the impression that they would be returning to Scotland in July to back another Parnes act, Dickie Pride, but the tour never materialized.

The journey home was miserable. The group were exhausted and broke. Tensions between "the boys" and Tommy Moore had grown worse since the accident. By this stage he would only talk to Stuart, totally ignoring the others.

To celebrate the return of "his boys" from their first tour, Allan Williams promoted them to the regular Monday night spot at the Jacaranda club. Payment would be in the form of free drinks of Coke and plates of beans-on-toast.

June 1960

As well as the regular Monday night sessions at The Jacaranda, the group was also by now playing regular Saturday night dances at the College Of Art. In fact various members of the Student Union soon regarded them as "the college band". Two members of the Union's social committee were particularly influential in this regard, Bill Harry and Stuart Sutcliffe.

Their influence also extended to them being able to use Student Union cash to "advance" the group sufficient funds "*to enable them to buy an amplifier which they could use, not only at school dances, but wherever they played.*[139]" The amp was never returned to the college, nor did The Beatles ever repay the loan.

It was also probably around this time that the group had their first experience of soft-drugs, other than their regular and prodigious alcohol consumption. On the evening of their first Jacaranda performance they were joined on stage by beat poet Royston Ellis, who was performing at Liverpool University. He proceeded to "perform" several of his poems with musical accompaniment from The Silver Beatles. After the gig he was invited back to the Gambier Terrace apartment. Here he introduced at least John and Stuart to Benzedrine, which was obtained by opening a Vicks Inhaler and chewing on the strip inside.

Shortly after this Paul was invited to an art college party with John. At the party a student with a goatee beard and striped T-shirt was hunched over a guitar singing what sounded like a French song. Soon after Paul began to work on a comical imitation to amuse his friends. It remained a party piece with nothing but Charles Azanavour style Gallic groaning for years afterwards. In 1965 John persuaded Paul to put some lyrics to the tune which was transformed into MICHELLE.

Regular gigs around Liverpool were also now part of the slightly renamed "Silver Beatles" schedule. The first gig after their return from Scotland was on the 2nd June at The Neston Institute replacing Cass & The Cassanovas who were now on the Billy Fury tour.

The local paper, The Hoylake News & Advertiser, in a preview article printed while the group was still in Scotland on May 27th commented that "*In their* (The Cassanovas) *place the teenagers of Neston and district will be able to dance to the music of The Silver Beetles (sic). This new five-piece group has made a terrific impact on Merseyside, pulling in capacity houses wherever they appear.*"

A review of this performance appeared in the Heswell and Neston edition of The Birkenhead News.

> *A Liverpool rhythm group "The Beatles," made their debut at The Neston Institute on Thursday night when north-west promoter, Mr. Les Dodds, presented three and a half hours of rock 'n' roll.*
>
> *The five strong group, which has been pulling in capacity houses on Merseyside, comprises three guitars, bass and drums.*
>
> *John Lennon, the leader, plays one of the three rhythm guitars, the other guitarists being Paul Ramon and Carl Harrison. Stuart De Stael plays the bass and the drummer is Thomas Moore. They all sing, either together, or as soloists.*
>
> *Recently they returned from a Scottish tour, staring Johnny Gentle, and are looking forward to a return visit in a month's time.*
>
> *Among the theatres they have played at are the Hippodrome, Manchester, the Empire, Liverpool and the Pavilion, Aintree.*

This review was the one furnished by John years later to prove his lack of stage name. Paul, Stuart and George were still using theirs. In it the group is referred to as "The Beatles" for the first time in print.* Why this version of the name was used has never

---

* *Although this was the first time that this group had been referred to in print as "The Beatles," it isn't the first recorded use of the name for a group of musicians. During the demolition of a house in New York in 1965 a dance card was found advertising a dance to be held at Perkins Hall, New York on Tuesday April 9, 1879 with "Music by The Beatles, full orchestra."*

been resolved, maybe the reporter had got the name from either Stuart or John, or maybe he just didn't hear the "Silver" part.

Two days later they played a gig at Groverner Ballroom, Groverner Road, Liskard, Wallasey, Cheshire. The Groverner, like the Neston Institute, was operated by local dance promoter Les Dodd under the "Paramount Enterprises" banner. Dodd had been promoting "strict tempo" ballroom dances at the Groverner and the Neston Institute since 1936. By 1960 he realized that beat bands were attracting large crowds and approached Allan Williams who suggested he book "The Silver Beatles." Other sources suggest it was Williams who approached him looking for a venue for his new charges. Pay was £10 (£1 to Williams, £1 for a bouncer and the rest split between the band members). Gigs at Dodds' venues ran from 8.00pm till midnight, admission was 3 shillings. They returned to the Groverner Ballroom on the 6th, this time sharing a bill with "Gerry & The Pacemakers."

The next gig at a Les Dodd's run event proved to a traumatic experience for all involved. At The Neston Institute on the 9th. One researcher[140] claims that a 16 year old boy was "stomped" to death by a gang of Teddy Boys right in front of the stage and the performing Silver Beatles. However this story has never been verified.

Whatever the reason, for the long-suffering Tommy Moore this was one gig too many and he didn't turn up for the next show on the 11th at the Groverner Ballroom. As a gag John asked if anyone in the audience fancied playing the drums. The only person who wanted to take John up on his offer was a well-known local thug called Ronnie. John expected his "guest" to play around for few minutes and leave, but Ronnie insisted on sitting in with the group for the whole set.

Tommy Moore also failed to show for the gig at The Jacaranda on the 13th. Allan Williams, Paul and John headed to the bottle works and tried to persuade their reluctant drummer to climb down off his forklift truck and rejoin the group. Despite their pleas, Tommy refused, preferring the stability of his "real job." The Silver Beatles were once more without a drummer.

The remainder of the month they struggled on without a drummer and alternating gigs at The Neston Institute on the 16th, 23rd and 30th with dates at The Groverner on the 18th and 25th.

For the last gig of the month at The Neston Institute, Paul was sporting a new guitar. With John and George both getting new guitars the previous November and Stuart's purchase in January, he must have felt he was due a change of instrument. So on the 30th he made the dutiful trip to Hessy's and signed a hire-purchase agreement for a Rosetta Solid 7 electric guitar. This was a great looking instrument with a semi-hollow double cutaway body.

While The Silver Beatles were working nearly every night and building a strong local reputation, perhaps the most significant event this month that had a long term impact on their future didn't even involve them.

Unknown to Allan Williams "The Royal Caribbean Steel Band" had abandoned The Jacaranda for a gig in the German port city of Hamburg. They had changed their name after Lord Woodbine left the band to become Allan William's business partner.

How the band came to land a Hamburg gig is something of a mystery. However Casey Jones, leader of Cass & The Cassanovas always maintained that he used the Jacaranda's phone after hours to contact promoter Bruno Koschmider in Hamburg and that one day Allan Williams intercepted the call and took over all the Hamburg contacts. If this is true, it's not inconceivable that The Royal intercepted a late night call and found themselves talked into a gig in Germany. However, as Williams didn't contact Koschmider until the following month this is unlikely.

Allan William's more plausible explanation is that "*some German seamen came* (into the club*) and told the band* (Royal Caribbean*) that they would get plenty of work in Hamburg.*[141]" Other variations on this theme is that some German seamen had seen the band playing at the Jac and recommended them to a Hamburg booking agent on their return home. Whatever the reason, the arrival of the Jac's house band in Hamburg would be key to the future of The Beatles.

July 1960

With his old band now playing in Germany, Allan William's business "partner" and associate Lord Woodbine suggested that the two entrepreneurs consider another business opportunity. In early July they opened an unlicensed club called the "New Cabaret Artists Club" at 174a Upper Parliament Street. Despite the high sounding address and club name, this was in fact an illegal strip club located in the cellar of an old run down Victorian house.

The "star" turn at Allan Williams' new venture was a buxom dancer from Manchester who went by the name of "Janice." As part of her contract she demanded a live backing band rather than dance to the usual records. This proved to be a problem as the club drew in most of its audience at lunchtime, when the local businessmen took a break from the daily office grind, to enjoy the spectacle of another sort of grind entirely.

As most of the local cabaret backing bands were amateur and only worked in the evenings, Williams needed to find a bunch of musicians who were available during the day. The answer was waiting for him at The Jacaranda—The Silver Beatles.

Alan Williams offered them a wage of 10 shillings a day for two twenty-minute sets. It wasn't much, but it was better than beans-on-toast. They took the gig. When they arrived at the club "Janice" gave them a set of sheet music for her usual backing numbers. Music by Beethoven and Khachaturian. It was meaningless to a group of teenagers who couldn't read a note of music. In fact The Beatles never formally learnt how to read music notation during their time together.

They agreed to play a set of instrumental numbers they did know. Janice danced to the accompaniment of tunes such as "SUMMERTIME," "BEGIN THE BEGINE," "HARRY LIME THEME" FROM THE THIRD MAN, "MOONGLOW," "THEME FROM PICNIC," "SEPTEMBER SONG," and "IT'S A LONG WAY FROM TIPPERARY."

The whole experience was an eye-opener for the teenagers. Paul later recalled *"John, George, Stu and I used to play in a strip club backing*

Janice The Stripper. At the time we wore little lilac, or purple, jackets, or something like that. Well we played behind Janice and naturally looked at her, everybody looked at her, just sort of normal. At the end of the act she would turn around and . . . well, we were all young lads, we'd never seen anything like it before, and we all blushed . . . four blushing red faced lads.[142]"

Around the same time as he was involved in the "New Cabaret Artists Club" Lord Woodbine also tried opening a business of his own. Called the "New Colony Club" it too was located in the cellar of an even more derelict house at 80 Berkely Street. The seedy little club soon became another place to spend long hours in, hanging about doing nothing in particular. In exchange for being allowed to stay The Silver Beatles would occasionally perform an informal afternoon session to help out their pal "Woodie."

With his new club underway, Allan Williams turned his attention to the next opportunity that had presented itself—Hamburg.

To Williams it seemed an obvious conclusion that if the Royal Caribbean steel band was going down well, there may be an opening for all the emerging rock groups to play in Germany. And, of course, he could set himself up as their sole representative. In Germany, as in Britain, rock 'n' roll was starting to replace jazz as the predominant popular music. The German promoters were keen to book rock 'n' roll acts into their clubs, but bringing stars over from America would be too expensive. Hiring young British groups who were playing American rock numbers would be a lot cheaper. Allan Williams saw an opportunity.

Asking to borrow the tape recorder that John had himself "borrowed" from the Art College*, Williams taped performances by several of the local rock 'n' roll groups and headed for Germany.

How Allan Williams found club owner Bruno Koschmider is something of a mystery. Some sources say he went looking for Koschmider, others that he just stumbled into the first club he found and that happened to be Koschmider's club Der Kaiserkellar.

---

* *Like the amp, the tape deck was never returned, and Stuart was later accused of stealing it.*

Alan Williams was determined to play his precious tape for the German club owner and after several attempts managed to set it up so he could let the Germans' hear just how good the Liverpool bands were. The tape was full of static hum, and nothing else.

Embarrassed Williams returned to Liverpool, but Bruno Koschmider was intrigued by all this talk of British rock bands. He set out for the one British city he knew—London and the 2Is (pronounced "two-eyes") Club where British Elvis-wannabe Tommy Steele had been "discovered" a few years earlier.

Here Koschmeider met a keyboard player called Iain Haines, formerly of the Alex Harvey band, who convinced Koschmider that he had a band called "The Jets"—a name he made up on the spur of the moment, and signed a contract. After the German promoter left, Haines hastily formed "The Jets" from among his friends who happened to be in the bar at the time. "The Jets", which included a singer called Tony Sheridan, became the first British rock-n-roll group to play in Hamburg. Sheridan would become instrumental in The Beatles getting their first professional recording contract in Germany the following year as his backing group.

While the "Silver Beatles" may have been spending their days hanging around Allan Williams' and Lord Woodbine's clubs, they were still playing regular evening gigs at their usual city wide venues.

Despite the loss of Tommy Moore, they struggled on without a drummer, and John never repeated his open invitation to anyone in the crowd who "fancied a bash."

For their first gig of the month, on the 2nd at The Groverner Ballroom, they were reunited with Johnny Gentle. Gentle was back in his hometown visiting family and decided to take in the gig by his old backing group. Part way through the evening he had joined them on-stage.

Their last gig as a drummer-less foursome was on the 7th July at the Wirral Institute. After the gig the group was, as usual, hanging around The Jacaranda when they heard the noise of drumming from across the street.

Alan Williams and the boys went in search of the mystery

drummer shouting in the street for him to show himself. The figure that emerged from the building opposite The Jac was Norman Chapman, a picture framer and restorer by trade.

Chapman was an amateur drummer who had taken to practicing in the office where he worked after hours rather than disturb his family at home. He was immediately offered a spot in the group and made his debut as a member of The Silver Beatles on the 9th at the Groverner ballroom.

They played the Groverner again on the 16th and the 23rd of the month. The fights between various factions of the audience were starting to get worse. Difficult to comprehend as it seems now, most of the audience didn't go to listen to The Silver Beatles play. They came to dance, and some came to fight. The slightest insult, perceived or imagined, was enough to spark a bloody confrontation between rival gangs of Teddy Boys.

While the Teddy Boys represented one threat to authority in the Britain of 1960, the other main concern for the Establishment, as far as teenagers were concerned, was the scourge of The Beatniks.

On the 24th July a national newspaper, The Sunday People, ran a full page article on "The Beatnik Horror." The accompanying photograph showed the squalid conditions that such arty teenagers lived in. The residence in question was none other than the interior of 3 Gambier Terrace, occupied by art college students, Mr. John Lennon and Mr. Stuart Sutcliffe.

In fact John and Stuart kept the spacious flat generally clean and tidy. A few weeks previously Alan William's had learnt the newspaper was running a series of articles on "beatniks" and "dropouts" from journalists that frequented the Jacaranda. They mentioned the paper was on the lookout for a typical "beatnik pad" to photograph. Alan William's volunteered 3 Gambier Terrace and persuaded John and Stuart to agree. Before the photo-shoot Williams deliberately made the flat look scruffy and untidy.

The day the article appeared in the national press, Williams was not in Liverpool but in London with another group he'd taken under his wing, Derry & The Seniors.

According to Allan Williams the trip was instigated by a call from Larry Parnes the previous day canceling a booking for Derry & The Seniors. Group leader Howard Casey was so upset that he threatened Williams with violence. Williams promised to drive to London straight away and get them a gig.

The first logical stop was the 2Is where he managed to get them a few minutes of stage time. Scanning the audience Williams was amazed to spot Bruno Koschmider sat at the back of the room.

Unknown to Williams, "The Jets" had been a big hit in the Hamburg clubs and Koschmider had returned to London to look for more acts. The last person that he expected to meet was the "man from Liverpool." After their short stage performance, Koschmider was so impressed enough by The Seniors to offer them a contract immediately. They left for Hamburg the next day. Of course he may have signed them just as an act of recognition for the part that Williams played in sparking his business interest in British rock 'n' roll bands.

Whatever the reason, Derry & The Seniors were the first Liverpool band to play in Hamburg. Many others would soon follow them.

Back in Liverpool, two distinct, yet separate, events would take The Silver Beatles once more crashing down and looking like they were going nowhere.

On the 30th July the group once again played at The Groverner Ballroom. The violence was the worst it had ever been and the organizers lost control. The local council immediately banned promoter Les Dodds from holding anymore "beat" concerts*. The council dance halls could now only be used for ballroom dancing. The Silver Beatles had lost their two most regular venues, The Groverner Hall and The Neston Institute. Plus the only promoter that was giving them regular work was now banned from employing them.

To add to the group's misery, new drummer Norman Chapman had received his call-up papers for National Service. He had to leave for basic training and was posted to Kenya.

---

* *The ban on rock-n-roll didn't last too long and The Beatles played the venue three more times during 1961*

Chapman was in one of the last batch of British youths drafted under National Service. The practice was dropped in December 1960. If it had carried on just a few months longer it's a strong possibility that John and Paul would have been drafted and The Beatles would never have emerged as the group it did.

"The Silver Beatles" were back to being a foursome, with no drummer and no prospect of regular work. In the interim Paul, already showing signs of his musical diversity, would occasionally sit behind the skins when a drummer was needed.

The lack of a permanent drummer had also lost them the opportunity of two further tours as backing group for a member of the Larry Parnes stable. The gig for a second Johnny Gentle tour was passed to Cass & The Casanovas, and they also missed out on a booking to back singer Dickie Pride on his inaugural tour.

August 1960

Salvation for The Silver Beatles arrived at The Jacaranda on the 2nd August. It came in the form of a letter from Bruno Koschmider to Allan Williams asking if he could supply a group for a new club he was opening called The Indra.

Williams first thought was to offer it to Liverpool's most popular group of the time, Rory Storm and The Hurricanes. Although not their manager, Williams thought by arranging for the group known for its energetic showmanship, he would make a good impression on the Germans and it could lead to further business. Rory, already committed to the summer season at Butlins, turned the Hamburg trip down.

Next on Williams' list was Gerry & The Pacemakers, but the home loving group didn't want to go abroad. In desperation Williams turned to the group that spent most of its time hanging around his coffee bar. He told The Silver Beatles that the gig was theirs, with one stipulation. They had to find a drummer willing to go to Hamburg with them before the scheduled August 16th departure date. Given the group's track record at finding, and retaining, drummers this seemed like an impossible task.

George recalls, *"Allan Williams came and said "OK lads you've got this job in Germany. But he's asked for a 5 piece band." At that point Paul was the drummer because our other drummers didn't show up. That's when I said I know this guy, Pete Best, who'd had a drum kit for Christmas*[143]*."*

With the usual Groverner Ballroom gig cancelled, due to complaints about the noise and almost inevitable fighting from local residents, the group spent the evening of the 6th August at "The Casbah" watching Ken Brown & Pete Best's group The Blackjacks. By coincidence, this was the group's last performance as Ken was moving to London.

Pete Best recalls *"The former Quarrymen (sic) had started drifting back to The Casbah after their Scottish tour. George was the first to pop in, sometimes alone, sometimes with his brother Peter. The rest followed. By now I was the proud owner of a smart looking new kit in blue mother of pearl."*[144]

Pete's new kit was an expensive item from the Rusworth's Music store. The center piece was a large 26 inch bass drum, the standard size was 22 inches, which would contribute to Pete's distinctive driving drumming sound. This was complemented by a snare, top rack tom and floor tom as well as hi-hat and crash symbols.

A few days after the last Blackjack's gig, Pete Best received a call from Paul. *"How'd you like to come to Hamburg with The Beatles"*

Pete was asked to come down for an audition. This may have been a ploy by Paul to cover the fact that they were in desperate need of a drummer, as no one else was considered or auditioned.

Pete Best and his sparkling new Blue Pearl Premiere drum kit arrived to audition at the Wyvern Club on the 12th August. John was the only one there to listen to him. John suggested that rather than wait for the others Pete should start. He recalls playing *Ramrod*, by the end of which George and Stuart had arrived. After another couple of numbers Paul arrived and they all had a jam session playing SHAKIN ALL OVER. Pete also recalls that Allan Williams popped in towards the end of the audition but didn't really take that much notice of what was going on.

Pete Best: "*I blasted off six numbers. All standard stuff, 12-bar blues and all that. The consensus was 'you're in Pete.' And that was it.*[145]"

The new five-piece group debuted with a couple of gigs at The Jacaranda just to teach Pete the basic song list and practice a few of the Lennon-McCartney originals.

As well as a drummer, they had at last settled on a permanent name—THE BEATLES.

But, before they could leave, they had to first convince their parents that they should be allowed to go to Hamburg. John's Aunt Mimi knew that his art studies were almost a thing of the past by this point and reluctantly allowed him to pursue his dream. Stuart was scheduled to go on a year's sabbatical from College anyway, while George's parents gave their permission and some practical advice. His father told him to boil the water before using it, while his mother made some scones for the journey. But, Paul had the greatest problems, first enlisting the aid of his younger brother in pleading his case. When that failed Allan Williams was brought in. It is perhaps a sign of how good a salesman and talker he was that even though he could never get Paul's name right (calling him "John" all the way through his pitch), he successfully sold the skeptical Jim McCartney on the idea of steady wages and the opportunity for his son to "experience new, meaningful horizons."

On the 15th August Allan Williams wrote to Bruno Koschmider informing him that "The Beatles" would be leaving Liverpool the next day to take up residence in Hamburg. The news was greeted less than enthusiastically by Howey Casey of Derry & The Seniors. He complained that "*sending a bum group like The Beatles*" would ruin the chances of further Hamburg gigs for the other Liverpool bands. With a nice touch of irony, Casey would go on to be a member of Paul's post-Beatles group, Wings, in the mid 1970s.

The following day, the 16th August 1960, Lord Woodbine recalls that "*The five boys, Allan, his wife Beryl, myself and Allan's brother-in-law all piled into this little van for the trip. Allan and I shared the driving so we got the good seats. I don't know how comfortable it was for the ones in the back.*[146]"

The old green and cream Austin van had been decorated with the name "THE BEATLES' crudely made from strips of newspaper by John and stuck on the sides. In the boy's suitcases were new "costumes" of black crewneck sweaters and short hounds-tooth jackets for which Allan Williams had advanced them £15 each against an IOU signed by Stuart and Paul.

The long journey took them from Liverpool to Harwich and then by ferry to The Hook Of Holland. Entry into continental Europe was arranged on student visas, as Allan Williams didn't have the time to obtain the correct work permits for them.

On the road through Holland they stopped at the Arnhem War Memorial and had their photograph taken by Barry Chang, Allan's brother-in-law.

In the photo, Paul, George, Pete and Stuart are stood in front of the prophetic words "THEIR NAMES LIVETH EVERMORE."

John stayed in the van.

36 hours after leaving Liverpool, The Beatles arrived at The Indra Club at 34 Grosse Frenhiet Strasse in Hamburg.

Over the next three years in Hamburg, and back in Liverpool's Cavern club, The Beatles would refine the unique energetic style that would eventually change the world of popular music and inspire generations to come.

But that's a whole other story.

WHATEVER HAPPENED TO . . .?

KEN BROWN
Quarry Men—August 1959—Guitar

After splitting from The Quarry Men over the "fifteen shillings incident" Ken stayed on as a regular performer at The Casbah club, forming The Blackjacks with Pete Best. They stayed together as the resident group for about a year until August 1960 when Ken moved to London.

Ken has remained in London ever since and has recently contributed to a book about the Casbah Club, "The Beatles: The True Beginnings," and is now working on his own memoirs of his Quarry Men days, "Some Other Guy."

NORMAN CHAPMAN
The Beatles—June 1960—Drums

After completing his National Service tour of duty in the Army, stationed in Kenya, Norman returned to Liverpool where he eventually joined a group called The In Crowd who had a couple of minor hits.

In the mid-sixties Norman left Liverpool and ended up as a teacher at a boys public school in the South of England

ROD DAVIS
Quarry Men—October 1956 to June 1957—Banjo

Rod Davis left The Quarry Men in the summer of 1957 in

order to concentrate on his school studies. His interest in jazz lead to a spot playing the guitar with a jazz trio, also made up of ex-Quarry Bank pupils.

The most academic of The Quarry Men he went on to study modern languages at Cambridge. After Cambridge Rod moved to Germany where he taught English. Returning to Liverpool he taught French and Spanish until the end of the 1960s. He later moved onto organizing safaris and adventure holidays. In the 1980s he became a lecturer on tourism before retiring in 1996 to concentrate on writing and translating.

Rod retained his life-long interest in jazz and country music, being a proponent of the "bluegrass" style including playing at Britain's top bluegrass festival as a member of the "Bluegrass Ramblers." Rod has also become a Champion Windsurfer.

In 1992 Rod linked up with other ex-Quarry Men John "Duff" Lowe and Len Garry and recorded a few tunes at the Amadeus Studios in Liverpool and cut a CD entitled "Open For Engagements". The re-formed "Quarrymen" have been a regular feature at Beatles conventions around the world ever since.

On July 6th 1997, Rod arranged for Colin Hanton, Len Garry, Pete Shotton and Eric Griffiths to join him to play a gig at St. Peter's Church Hall in Woolton to commemorate the 40th anniversary of the historic meeting between Paul McCartney and John Lennon.

Since then Rod has become the driving force and custodian of The Quarry Men legacy over the last few years, organizing reunion gigs, tours, CDs and maintaining the official Quarrymen web site.

LEN GARRY
Quarry Men—November 1956 to
August 1958—Tea Chest Bass

During Len's hospitalization with Tubercular Meningitis, The Quarry Men developed and matured and he never really felt like he belonged anymore. Although invited by Paul and John to join them for a gig at The Casbah, Len declined and turned instead to developing a career in architecture, becoming articled to a firm of Liverpool architects.

Len left Liverpool in 1971 for Somerset. Maintaining his love of music and singing he took part in a touring version of the rock gospel musical "Come Together." In 1987 Len emigrated to New Zealand for a short while, but couldn't settle and returned to Liverpool in 1988 where he still lives.

Len also wrote of his time as a member of The Quarry Men in his book, JOHN, PAUL & ME: BEFORE THE BEATLES, published in 1997.

Len is now the lead vocalist in The Quarrymen, at last taking on the role that he coveted back in 1956.

ERIC GRIFFITHS
Quarry Men—October 1956 to March 1958—Guitar

Eric left The Quarry Men after George Harrison joined. Suddenly overwhelmed by guitarists Eric was asked to consider switching to bass but he couldn't afford the new guitar and amp necessary to make the switch, so left.

At the time that Eric left The Quarry Men he was serving an engineering apprenticeship at Napier Engineering in Liverpool. He left Napier's after only six months and joined the Merchant Navy where he progressed to the rank of Second Officer. Coming ashore to get married he held a number of jobs eventually joining the Prison Service as a work study officer. Moving to Scotland in the 1970's he rose to a senior management post in the Prison Service. Retired from the Prison Service, he currently owns a chain of dry cleaning stores in Edinburgh.

Eric had not played the guitar since leaving the original Quarry Men in 1958, but was persuaded to join the re-formed Quarrymen for the 1997 reunion gig, and is now a semi-regular with them.

COLIN HANTON
Quarry Men—October 1956 to January 1959—Drums

After storming out of the Quarry Men, disgusted at their unprofessional and drunken conduct during a gig, Colin concentrated on completing his apprenticeship. Becoming a successful upholsterer he set up his own upholstery business in nearby Runcorn.

Colin never used the drums again, and the original Quarry Men drum set lay untouched on top of his wardrobe for many years, until the 1997 reunion gig at Woolton. Since then Colin has played several gigs with The Quarrymen and his famous drum set has been on display at several museums.

JOHN "DUFF" LOWE
Quarry Men—May 1957 to August 1958—Piano

After leaving Liverpool, John headed for the South West of England and became a prosperous stock broker living just outside of Bristol.

He had pretty much forgotten about his Quarry Men days until he realized that he was still in possession of the original acetate from their only recording session. He eventually sold it back to Paul McCartney for an undisclosed sum.

While he played on the "Open For Engagements" CD, John has not played at any of the re-formed Quarrymen live dates.

TOMMY MOORE
The Beatles—May 1960 to June 1960—Drums

After leaving The Silver Beatles at the culmination of their Scottish tour, Tommy Moore returned to his job as a forklift driver at Garston Bottle Works. Despite several pleas by the boys to rejoin them, he stayed secure in his day job. Tommy eventually moved on to a position with Liverpool City Council and played drums with a local jazz combo on occasional evenings. Tommy's life was tragically cut short in the early 1970s when he died following an epileptic fit at the age of forty-seven.

PETE SHOTTON
Quarry Men—October 1956 to June 1957—Washboard.

John Lennon's oldest and best friend left the Quarry Men after an argument with John. Despite this Pete and John remained close and loyal friends.

After graduating from the Police Academy Pete was assigned a beat in one of the toughest areas of Liverpool. After nine months of night duty, Pete had had enough and resigned from the force. He went into partnership with the owner of the Old Dutch Café, a late night coffee bar that was often frequented by the leather clad early Beatles.

Pete and John always stayed in touch and at the height of Beatlemania Pete was often present at key moments in the Beatles story. In 1963 John generously gave Pete the funds to open a betting shop (Pete's long time ambition). Pete never found a suitable location and spent the money on other things. John didn't seem to mind and told Pete to look around for a business venture that would "make him a lot of money." The result was that John ended up giving Pete the funds to buy a supermarket in Hampshire not too far from John's home in Weybridge. Pete became a frequent companion for John through the mid to late 60s.

In 1967 John formerly bought Pete into the Beatles fold to manage the newly opened Apple Boutique. It didn't take Pete too long to become disillusioned with the operations at Apple. He left the boutique and became John's personal assistant and companion until Yoko Ono came on the scene.

Pete then moved on to a number of other business ventures having sold the supermarket. After John moved to New York Pete only saw him only once more.

Pete wrote of his friendship with John in his book "JOHN LENNON IN MY LIFE" published in 1983.

Pete founded the "Fatty Arbuckle's" restaurant chain in 1995 and opened several across the UK, including one in Liverpool. He sold the chain in 2001 and now lives the life of a multi-millionaire tax recluse moving between his boat and a house in Ireland.

Pete has become a regular member of the re-formed Quarrymen and has swapped his washboard and tea-chest bass for a bass guitar.

BILL SMITH
Quarry Men—September 1956 to October 1956—Tea Chest Bass

Bill holds the honor of being the first person to join John Lennon's group and the first to leave it, his tenure as a member of the Quarry Men being just a few weeks. After leaving Quarry Bank school Bill Smith joined the merchant navy. After a few years of life at sea he emigrated to South Africa where he lived until recently.

He returned to Liverpool in 2002 and has since played a one-off gig with the re-formed Quarrymen.

IVAN VAUGHAN
Quarry Men—September 1956— Occasional Tea Chest Bass.

"Ivy," the boy who introduced Paul McCartney to John Lennon went on to became a school teacher and university lecturer. During the height of Beatlemania he remained in close contact with his good friend Paul. Ivan traveled to America with The Beatles and was present for some of the Sgt Pepper sessions

In his 30s Ivan was diagnosed with Parkinson's Disease. As it is unusual for anyone to be diagnosed at such a young age, Ivan decided to become a human guinea pig for research into the disease. Ivan's courageous stand became the subject of a BBC documentary. Following his TV appearance Ivan became one of the first vocal advocates for people suffering from the disease, and he wrote a book "Ivan: Living With Parkinson's Disease" that was published in 1986.

Ivan died in 1994, his death touched Paul McCartney so deeply that he started to write poetry for the first time since his childhood.

NIGEL WHALLEY
Quarry Men—September 1956 to December 1957—Manager

Nigel was distraught at witnessing the death of John Lennon's mother in a traffic accident and soon afterwards left Liverpool for good.

He eventually achieved his ambition to become a golf-pro and became the resident professional at a club in Kent in the south east of England.

EVOLUTION OF A BAND

The following table is an attempt to chronicle every combination of line up and name change in the group that would eventually emerge as THE BEATLES.

Many of the changes, especially in the early Quarry Men days, were arbitrary and went undocumented. This table has been compiled by comparing the various published accounts.

DATE (name)	Guitar	Guitar	Guitar	Bass	Drums	Washboard	Banjo	Piano
Sep-56	John Lennon					Pete Shotton		
Sep-56	John Lennon			Bill Smith (tea chest)		Pete Shotton		
Oct-56	John Lennon		Eric Griffiths	Bill Smith (tea chest)		Pete Shotton		
Oct-56	John Lennon		Eric Griffiths	Bill Smith (tea chest)		Pete Shotton	Rod Davis	
Oct-56 Blackjacks	John Lennon		Eric Griffiths	Bill Smith (tea chest)	Colin Hanton	Pete Shotton	Rod Davis	
Oct-56 Quarry Men	John Lennon		Eric Griffiths	Bill Smith (tea chest)	Colin Hanton	Pete Shotton	Rod Davis	
Nov-56 Quarry Men	John Lennon		Eric Griffiths	Len Garry (tea chest)	Colin Hanton	Pete Shotton	Rod Davis	
May-57 Quarry Men	John Lennon		Eric Griffiths	Len Garry (tea chest)	Colin Hanton	Pete Shotton	Rod Davis	John Lowe (?)
Jun-57 Quarry Men	John Lennon		Eric Griffiths	Len Garry (tea chest)	Colin Hanton	Pete Shotton	Rod Davis	
Sep-57 Quarry Men	John Lennon		Eric Griffiths	Len Garry (tea chest)	Colin Hanton			
Oct-57 Quarry Men	John Lennon	Paul McCartney	Eric Griffiths	Len Garry (tea chest)	Colin Hanton			
Mar-58 Quarry Men	John Lennon	Paul McCartney	Eric Griffiths / George	Len Garry (tea chest)	Colin Hanton			John Lowe

Jun-58 Quarry Men	John Lennon	Paul McCartney	George Harrison	Len Garry (tea chest)	Colin Hanton		
Aug-58 Quarry Men	John Lennon	Paul McCartney	George Harrison		Colin Hanton		John Lowe
Dec-58 Rainbows?	John Lennon	Paul Mccartney	George Harrison		Colin Hanton		
Feb-59 Quarry Men	John Lennon	Paul McCartney	George Harrison				
Aug-59 Quarry Men	John Lennon	Ken Brown	George Harrison	Paul McCartney			
Oct-59 Johnny & The Moondogs	John Lennon	Paul McCartney	George Harrison				
Jan-60 Johnny & The Moondogs	John Lennon	Paul McCartney	George Harrison	Stuart Sutcliffe			
Mar-60 Beatals	John Lennon	Paul McCartney	George Harrison	Stuart Sutcliffe			
Apr-60 Nerk Twins	John Lennon	Paul McCartney					
May-60 Silver Beatles	John Lennon	Paul McCartney	George Harrison	Stuart Sutcliffe	Tommy Moore		
May-60 Johnny Gentle & Silver Beetles	John Lennon	Paul McCartney	George Harrison	Stuart Sutcliffe	Tommy Moore		
Jun-60 Silver Beatles	John Lennon	Paul McCartney	George Harrison	Stuart Sutcliffe	Tommy Moore		
JULY 60 Silver Beats	John Lennon	Paul McCartney	George Harrison	Stuart Sutcliffe			
Jul-60 Silver Beatles	John Lennon	Paul McCartney	George Harrison	Stuart Sutcliffe	Norman Chapman		
Aug-60 Silver Beatles	John Lennon	Paul McCartney	George Harrison	Stuart Sutcliffe			
Aug-60 BEATLES	John Lennon	Paul McCartney	George Harrison	Stuart Sutcliffe	Pete Best		

THE MUSIC (1957-1960)

SONG TITLE	COMMENT	RECORDING
A WORLD WITHOUT LOVE	Early Lennon-McCartney piece written in 1959. A #1 hit for Peter & Gordon in 1964. No evidence that it was every played on stage or recorded.	
AIN'T SHE SWEET	Gene Vincent song performed by The Quarry Men with Jihn on lead vocal, stayed in Beatles set until 1962. Possibly the song that John Lennon was singing at a college lunch time that first drew Cynthia Powell to him.	The Early Tapes Of The Beatles, Beatles Anthology 1, (Beatles)
AIN'T THAT A SHAME	Fats Domino hit from 1955. Included in the Quarry Men set in 1958 and stayed in The Beatles play list until 1961	
ALL SHOOK UP	Elvis #1 hit in the UK added to the Quarry Men set in October 1957 with Paul on lead vocals.	
BABY LET'S PLAY HOUSE	Sung by The Quarry Men at the Woolton Fete and recorded	
BE BOP A-LULA	1956 Gene Vincent song that was a Quarry Men regular for John, and was still performed by The Beatles as late as 1962.	Rock N Roll (John)
BEGIN THE BEGUINE	1957 Pat Boone hit played by "The Silver Beetles" during their early 1960 gig as backing group for the stripper known as "Janice." Possibly sung by Paul	
BLUE MOON OF KENTUCKY	1954 Elvis hit added to the Quarry Men set in 1957 and stayed in Beatles set until 1961 with Paul on lead.	
BLUE SUEDE SHOES	A hit for both Carl Perkins and Elvis. Added to the Quarry Men set in 1957 and used through 1962. A favorite of John's.	Beatles Anthology 3 (Beatles), Plastic Ono Band – Live In Toronto 1969 (John)
BONY MORONIE	Larry Williams hit from 1957. A regular on stage from 1957 to 1962 with John on lead vocal.	
BOPPIN THE BLUES	Carl Perkins hit from 1956 added to The Quarry Men set in 1959 and used until 1962 with John on lead vocal.	
BYE BYE LOVE	Everly Brothers song sung as a duet by Paul and his brother Mike during their appearance in a talent show at Butlins holiday camp in 1957.	
CATHY'S CLOWN	Everly Brothers hit from early 1960 added to the Beatles set for later that year and used through 1962.	
CATSWALK	Early McCartney instrumental piece from Quarry Men days and played on stage through 1962. Later recorded by Chris Barber as "Catcall" in October 1967.	
CAYEENE	Early McCartney instrumental from the late 50s. A version was captured on the 1960s rehearsal tape but no note of a live performance has been found.	Beatles Anthology 1. (Beatles)
CLARABELLA	Originally recorded by The Jodimars in 1956, was added to The Beatles set in 1960 with Paul on lead vocals. Was used through till 1962.	Live At The BBC (Beatles)
C'MON EVERYBODY	Eddie Cochran hit from 1959 introduced into the Quarry Men set shortly afterwards and used through 1962.	
COME GO WITH ME	A hit for Del Viking that was sung by The Quarry Men from 1957 to 1959. This may have been the song John was singing when Paul McCartney first saw him on stage at the Woolton Fete	
CORRINE CORRINA	Ray Peterson hit from 1960 added to The Beatles set and used through 1962.	

133

CRYING WAITING HOPING	B-side to Buddy Holly's "Peggy Sue" added to The Beatles set in 1960 with George on lead vocals. One of the songs sung during their abortive Decca audition.	Live At The BBC (Beatles)
CUMBERLAND GAP	A skiffle standard recorded by Lonnie Donegan that reached #1 in the UK in 1957 and launched the skiffle craze. Like every other skiffle band, The Quarry Men included this in their set with John on lead. It was dropped in 1959 as the band moved more towards rock-n-roll.	
DANCE IN THE STREET	Gene Vincent hit from 1958 introduced into The Beatles set in 1960 and used till late 1962.	
DARKTOWN STRUTTERS BALL	Traditional song which charted in March 1960 sung by Joe Brown & The Bruvvers. Added to The Beatles set later in 1960.	
DIZZY MISS LIZZY	Hit for Larry Williams in 1958 added to the Beatles set in 1960. and used through 1965 with John on lead vocal.	Help, Live At The BBC (Beatles), Plastic Ono Band – Live In Toronto 1969, Lennon, (John),
DO YOU WANT TO DANCE	1958 Bobby Freeman hit added to The Quarry Men set the following year and used until 1962 with John on lead.	
DON'T BE CRUEL	1956 Elvis hit that was added to the Quarry Men set in 1959 and used until 1961, possibly with Paul on lead vocal.	
DON'T FORBID ME	Pat Boone hit from 1957 introduced into The Beatles set in 1960. Dropped by 1962.	
DON'T LET THE SUN CATCH YOU CRYIN'	Ray Charles number from 1960 included in The Beatles set for a short time that year with Paul on lead. (NOTE In 1964, Gerry & The Pacemakers charted with a different song under the same title.)	
DON'T YOU ROCK ME DADDYO	Early Lonnie Donegan skiffle number, part of The Quarry Men set from the early days.	
EVERYDAY	Buddy Holly hit from 1957 that was a standard from Quarry Men sets in 1957 through Beatles shows in 1962.	
FOOLS LIKE ME	1959 Jerry Lee Lewis hit first played live by The Silver Beatles in 1960 with John on lead and used through 1962.	
FRIEGHT TRAIN	Traditional American folk song. A skiffle hit in the UK for Chazz McDevit & Nancy Whiskery. Part of the Quarry Men set from 1957 to 1959 with John on lead vocals.	
GONE GONE GONE	Carl Perkins number from 1959 performed by The Beatles for a from 1960 to 1962.	
GOOD GOLLY MISS MOLLY	Little Richard hit from 1958, part of Quarry Men set with Paul on lead. Used until 1961.	
GOOD ROCKIN' TONIGHT	Elvis hit from 1954 part of The Quarry Men set from 1958 and used through 1962.	
GUITAR BOOGIE	Quarry Men regular guitar solo piece from 1957 to 1959, that Paul made a mess of on his debut with the band. Originally recorded by Arthur Smith And His Crackerjacks in 1946.	
HALLELUJAH I LOVE HER SO	1956 Ray Charles number made popular in the UK by Eddie Cochran in 1960 just prior to his death. Used in the Beatles set from 1960 onwards. The rehearsal tape made in 1960 is the only surviving recording of Stuart Sutcliffe's tenure with the band. (Note: The version on "The Beatles Live at the Star Club has Horst Fascher on lead vocals)	Beatles Anthology 1 (Beatles) Beatles Live at the Star Club. (Beatles)
HARRY LIME THEME	Originally recorded in 1949 and used in the movie "The Third Man". Made popular in 1960 when Chet Atkins recorded a new version Played by "The Silver Beetles" during their gig as backing group for the stripper known as "Janice"	
HEARTBREAK HOTEL	Elvis classic from 1956 and a regular for The Quarry Men from 1957 and used by The Beatles through 1961.	

HELLO LITTLE GIRL	Early Lennon piece from Quarry Men days. Hit for The Fourmost in 1963. This was the first song that John wrote solo at around age 18 (1958?). It was loosely based on a couple of old standards that Julia Lennon used to sing to him as a child. It was used by The Beatles during both their Decca and Paralaphone auditions and played on stage until 1962.	Beatles Anthology 1 (Beatles)
HEY DARLIN	An early McCartney-Harrison composition that was used occasionally between 1959 and 1960.	
HEY GOOD LOOKIN'	A Hank Williams' number later recorded by Gene Vincent and included in The Beatles set from 1960 to 62, possibly with John on lead..	
HIGH SCHOOL CONFIDENTIAL	Jerry Lee Lewis hit from 1958 included as part of Quarry Men set that year and used through 1961 with Paul on lead vocal.	
HOME	An early standard, part of The Quarry Men set from 1957 through 1960	
HONKY TONK BLUES	Hank Williams from 1952 added to The Quarry Men set in 1957 with John on lead and dropped in 1959 as the group moved to more rock than skiffle.	
HOT AS SUN	Early McCartney instrumental piece from Quarry Men days. Used on stage from 1957 to 1959. Included on Paul's first solo album in 1970.	McCartney (Paul)
HOUND DOG	Elvis hit from 1956 added to the Quarry Men set. Sung by John on the Quarry Men's debut at The Cavern on 7th August 1957. It's inclusion in what was billed as a "skiffle evening" lead to him being told to "cut out the bloody rock." Continued as part of The Beatles set until 1961.	John Lennon Live In New York City, Lennon, (John)
HULLY GULLY	Hit for The Olympics in 1959 and introduced into The Beatles set in 1960 and used through 1962.	The Beatles Live At The Star Club (Beatles)
I LOST MY LITTLE GIRL	Paul's first song, probably written in reaction to the death of his mother. Paul played this song to John after his first gig with The Quarry Men. It was included in The Quarry Men set from then on but was dropped just prior to them leaving for Hamburg. The Beatles never recorded the song but Paul eventually released it on his 1991 solo album "Unplugged"	Unplugged (McCartney, Paul)
I REMEMBER	Eddie Cochran hit from 1959 that was a part of the Beatles set from 1960 to early 1961.	
I'LL BE ON MY WAY	Early Lennon-McCartney piece written in 1959. Later recorded by Billy J. Kramer & The Dakotas. (NOTE no record exists of The Beatles performing this song prior to 1961)	Live At The BBC (Beatles)
I'LL CALL HER NAME	A possible early Lennon composition. According to John he wrote this "when there was no Beatles and no group" which seems to place it at pre March 57. But John didn't start to write until November 57. There is also no record of it being performed by the Quarry Men.	With The Beatles (Beatles)
I'LL FOLLOW THEM	An early Paul McCartney composition written at the age of 16 (possibly early 1959) while recovering from the 'flu.	
I'LL FOLLOW THE SUN	Written by Paul in February 1959 shortly after the death of Buddy Holly and performed regularly through 1961.	Beatles For Sale (Beatles)
I'M GONNA SIT RIGHT DOWN AND CRY (OVER YOU)	Elvis song from 1956 added to The Beatles set in early 1960 with John on lead vocal.	Live At The BBC (Beatles)
IN SPITE OF ALL THE DANGER	McCartney-Harrison composition from 1958 that was the first Beatles song recorded with John on lead vocal. Both as The Quarry Men and as The Beatles in Hamburg	Beatles Anthology 1 (Beatles)
IT'LL BE ME	Jerry Lee Lewis hit from 1957 added to The Quarry Men set in 1959 and used until 1961.	

IT'S A LONG WAY FROM TIPPERARY	Traditional tune played by "The Silver Beetles" during their gig as backing group for the stripper known as "Janice"	
IT'S SO EASY	Buddy Holly song, a regular part of the Quarry Men set in 1958 (also rehearsed by "Johnny & The Moondogs" for the Regional finals of Star Search in November 1959). Was a regular part of The Beatles set until 1962.	
IT WON'T BE LONG	An undeveloped composition that became the base for ANY TIME AT ALL on the Hard Day's Night album	Hard Day's Night (Beatles)
JAILHOUSE ROCK	Elvis hit that was a standard in The Quarry Men set from 1957 through 1960 with John on lead.	
JOHN HENRY	Traditional "skiffle" song, a hit for Lonnie Donegan and part of The Quarry Men set from the early days. Dropped in 1959.	
JOHNNY BE GOODE	Classic Chuck Berry number included in The Beatles set from 1959 with John on lead. Was a part of The Beatles set as late as 1964.	Live At The BBC (Beatles)
JUST FUN	Early (1957?) Lennon-McCartney piece from Quarry Men days that was never recorded, but played on stage through 1959.	
KANSAS CITY / HEY HEY HEY	Melody combining a Lieber and Stoller classic (Kansas City) with a Little Richard hit (Hey Hey Hey) part of Quarry Men set with Paul on lead.	Beatles For Sale, The Beatles Live At The Star Club. Early Tapes Of The Beatles, Live At The BBC, Beatles Anthology 1 (Beatles)
KEEP LOOKING THAT WAY	Early (1957) Lennon-McCartney piece from Quarry Men days. And played as part of live set through 1959.	
LAWDY MISS CLAWDY	Originally Lloyd Price hit from 1952, but made popular by Elvis in 1956. Part of The Quarry Men set from 1957 and a regular Beatles stage number through till 1962.	
LAZY RIVER	Gene Vincent hit from 1956 and included as part of The Beatles set from 1959 to 1961 with John on lead vocal.	
LEND ME YOUR COMB	Carl Perkins hit from 1957 that was added to the Quarry Men set almost immediately and used until 1962.	
LIKE DREAMERS DO	Early McCartney piece from Quarry Men days. And sung by The Beatles until 1962. Played as part of their Decca audition. A hit for The Applejacks in 1964.	Beatles Anthology 1 (Beatles)
LITTLE QUEENIE	Chuck Berry hit from 1959 that was introduced into The Beatles set in 1960 and used until 1963.	The Beatles Live At The Star Club (Beatles)
LOOKING GLASS	Early Lennon instrumental piece from Quarry Men days.	
LONG BLACK TRAIN	Version of "*Streamlined Train*" re-titled by John after he improvised a new section of lyrics/ Performed by The Quarry Men.	
LONG TALL SALLY	Little Richard hit for 1956, part of Quarry Men set from 1957 and still used by The Beatles as late as 1966 with Paul on lead This is the first number that Paul ever sang on stage during his performance at the Butlins talent show along side his brother Mike. It is also the first number he sang as a member of The Quarry Men. This song lasted longer on The Beatles play list than any other and is the only song to be used throughout their entire stage career.	Past Masters Vol. 1, Live At The BBC, Beatles Anthology 1 (Beatles)
LOOKING GLASS	Early Lennon-McCartney instrumental used as part of The Quarry Men set from 1957 till 1959.	
LOST JOHN	A skiffle standard used by The Quarry men in their early sets.	
LOVE ME DO	Early McCartney piece from Quarry Men days. Written in 58 while Paul was playing truant from school. The Beatles first single. Wasn't performed on stage until 1962	Please Please Me, Past Masters Vol. 1, Live At The BBC, Beatles Anthology 1 (Beatles)
LOVE ME TENDER	1956 hit for Elvis based on the traditional 1861 ballad. Included in The Beatles set in 1960 and 61 as a showcase for Stuart Sutcliffe – one of the few songs he sang.	

LOVE OF THE LOVED	Early Lennon-McCartney piece written in 1959. Part of The Quarry Men set from 1959 and played as part of the Decca Audition. Hit for Cilla Black in 1963.	
LOVING YOU	Another Elvis hit (from 1957) that was included in the 1960 set for Stuart Sutcliffe to take lead.	
LUCILLE	Little Richard hit from 1957 that was a standard part of The Quarry Men / Beatles set until 1962, introduced by Paul who sang lead. Paul was still performing this song as late as 1979 (Concert For Kampuchia).	Live At The BBC (Beatles)
MAGGIE MAE	Traditional Liverpool sea shanty about a famous local prostitute. Was a hit for The Vipers Skiffle Group in 1957. Introduced into the Quarry Men set from the start and regularly sung by The Beatles until 1963. A shortened version was eventually released on the 1969 "Let It Be" album – ironically their last.	Let It Be (Beatles)
MAILMAN BLUES	Lloyd Price composition from 1954 included as part of The Quarry Men's set between 1957 and 1959.	
MAYBE BABY	Buddy Holly hit from 1958 and a regular stage number until 1961.	
MAYBELLENE	1955 Chuck Berry hit that was a regular part of The Quarry Men set from 1959 to 1961 with John on lead vocal.	
MEAN WOMAN BLUES	Jerry Lee Lewis hit (or maybe song from the 1957 Elvis movie) included as part of Quarry Men set and stayed on the play list until 1962. Probably sung by John.	
MEMPHIS, TENNESSEE	Chuck Berry's 1959 hit was added to The Beatles set in 1960 with John on lead.	
MICHELLE	Untitled at this early stage, this was Paul's party piece done to poke fun at the pretensions of several art college students he'd met at a party.	Rubber Soul (Beatles)
MIDNIGHT SHIFT	A 1956 hit for Buddy Holly that was included in The Beatles set from 1960 to 1962.	
MIDNIGHT SPECIAL	Lonnie Donegan hit from 1956 included in the Quarry Men set in 1957 and used through 1960 when the group dropped all of its skiffle based songs.	
MISS ANN	Hit for Little Richard in 1956 and added to The Beatles set in 1960 with Paul on lead.	
MONEY (THAT'S WHAT I WANT)	This Barret Strong classic from 1959 was added to The Beatles set in 1960 and stayed as part of their regular act until 1964 with John on lead vocal.	
MOONGLOW	The theme from the 1956 movie "Picnic" played by The Silver Beetles during their 1960 gig as backing group for the stripper known as "Janice." May have also been part of The Quarrymen set from 1957 onwards.	
MOVIN' AND GROOVIN'	This Duane Eddy instrumental was a regular part of the groups set during its various incarnations in 1959 and 60.	
MYSTERY TRAIN	1955 hit for Elvis that was a regular Quarry Men number from 1957 to 1959 with John on lead.	
NO OTHER BABY	Hit for the skiffle group "The Vipers" in 1958. Introduced into The Quarry Men set later that year with John on lead vocals.	
NOTHIN SHAKEN' BUT THE LEAVES ON THE TREES	Hit for Eddie Fontaine in 1958 and introduced into The Beatles set in 1960 with George on lead.	Live At The BBC (Beatles)
ONE AFTER 909	Early Lennon piece from Quarry Men days. One of John's earliest compositions and a regular in both Quarry Men and Beatles sets until 1962. It was recorded by The Beatles in 1963 but not released until the Let It Be album in 1970.	Let It Be, Beatles Anthology 1 (Beatles)
OOH MY SOUL	Little Richard hit from 1958, part of The Beatles set from 1960 onwards with Paul on lead.	Live At The BBC (Beatles)
(LET'S HAVE A) PARTY	Elvis hit from 1957 added to The Quarry Men set that year and used through 1960 with John on lead vocal.	

PEGGY SUE	Buddy Holly hit from 1957. Included in the Quarry Men set that year with John on lead. Stayed a regular part of The Beatles set until 1962.	Rock N Roll (John)
PUTTIN' ON THE STYLE	Traditional skiffle song, hit for Lonnie Donegan in 1957, Sung by The Quarry Men at the Woolton Fete and recorded.	
RAILROAD BILL	Lonnie Donegan hit from 1956/57 included in the Quarry Men set in 1957 with John on lead.	
RAINING IN MY HEART	1959 hit for Buddy Holly and a regular part of The Beatles set from 59 until 1962, possibly with Paul on lead.	
RAMROD	Daune Eddy instrumental from 1958 and a part of The Quarry Men set from 1958 until 1960.	
RAUNCHY	George's famous audition piece and his solo "party piece" until 1960. This instrumental was originally a 1957 hit from Bill Justis	
READY TEDDY	1956 Little Richard hit that was part of The Beatles set from 1959 until 1961, featuring John on lead vocal.	
RAVE ON	1958 Buddy Holly hit performed by Johnny & The Moondogs during the Star Search finals in Manchester.	
RED SAILS IN THE SUNSET	First recorded by Joe Turner in 1959. The Beatles heard the Emile Ford version in 1960 and added it to their set.	
RIP IT UP	1956 Little Richard song that was added to the set in 1959 and used until 1961 with John on lead vocal.	
ROCK ISLAND LINE	Hit for Lonnie Donegan in 1956 that launched the skiffle craze. Like nearly every other skiffle group The Quarry Men included it in their set from the beginning and used it until 1959	
ROCK 'N' ROLL MUSIC	Chuck Berry's 1957 classic Performed by The Beatles from 1959 to 1966 with John on lead vocal. The "Backbeat" song.	
ROLL OVER BEETHOVEN	Chuck Berry hit from 1956 included in the Quarry Men set from the beginning with John on lead. It became a staple of The Beatles act right through to 1964, with George taking over the lead vocal from 61 onwards. There are numerous recorded versions with George on lead.	With The Beatles, Live At The BBC, Beatles Anthology 1, (Beatles)
SEARCHIN	Hit for The Coasters in 1957 and added to The Quarry Men set in 1958 and stayed on The Beatles play list until 1962 with Paul on lead. Played during the Decca audition.	Beatles Anthology 1. (Beatles)
SEND ME SOME LOVIN'	Little Richard hit from 1957, added to The Beatles set in 1959 with John on lead and used until 1962.	
SEPTEMBER SONG	1959 hit for Johnny Ray. Played by "The Silver Beetles" during their gig as backing group for the stripper known as "Janice"	
SHAKIN ALL OVER	No. 1 hit for British Rock-n-roll group Johnny Kidd & The Pirates in 1960. Included in The Beatles set almost immediately and played through till 1961.	
SHIMMY SHIMMY	A US hit for Bobby Freeman in 1960 and added to The Beatles set that year. Used until 1963.	
SHORT FAT FANNY	Hit for Larry Williams in 1957 and added to The Quarry Men set in 1958 with John on lead, used until 1961.	
SHOUT	Isley Brothers hit from 1959 and included in The Beatles set in 1960 and 1961. One of the rare songs where John, Paul & George sang harmony rather than one of them taking the lead vocal.	Beatles Anthology 1 (Beatles)
SILHOUETTE	Hit for The Rays in 1957 that was the inspiration for John's NO REPLY on the Beatles For Sale album.	
SLOW DOWN	Larry Williams song from 1958 included in The Beatles set from 1960 with John on lead. Used until 1963	Past Masters Vol. 1, Live At The BBC (Beatles)
SOMEWHERE OVER THE RAINBOW	The Judy Garland classic from The Wizard Of Oz. The Beatles incorporated a stylized haunting version of this song into their set after hearing Gene Vincent perform it at the Liverpool Stadium gig in 1960.	

SUMMERTIME	Gerswhin classic played by "The Silver Beetles" during their gig as backing group for the stripper known as "Janice". They were already playing a "rock" version after introducing it into The Quarry Men set in 1958 after hearing Gene Vincent's version.	
SURE TO FALL	Carl Perkins hit from 1956. Part of The Quarry Men set from 1957 and sung by The Beatles trough till late 62 with Paul on lead. Played during the Decca audition.	Live At The BBC, (Beatles)
SWEET LITTLE SIXTEEN	Chuck Berry hit from 1956. Part of The Quarry Men set from 1957 on with John on lead. A regular part of The Beatles set until 1962.	Live At The BBC, The Beatles Live At The Star Club (Beatles) Rock N Roll, Lennon, (John)
TEENAGE HEAVEN	Eddie Cochran hit from 1959 included in The Beatles set from 1960.	
TENNESSE	Carl Perkins recording from 1956. Part of Quarry Men set from the earliest days with John on lead. Part of The Beatles set until 1961.	
TEQUILA	1958 instrumental hit for The Champs. Played by the group during its various 1959 / 60 incarnations.	
THAT'S ALL RIGHT MAMA	Elvis hit (from 1954) Part of The Quarry Men set from 1957 and still used by The Beatles as late as 1963 with Paul on lead vocal.	Live At The BBC (Beatles)
THAT'LL BE THE DAY	Classic Buddy Holly hit and the first "rock-n-roll" number that John learned to play. Included in The Quarry Men set from 1957 until 1960. A-side of Quarry Men's first recording.	Beatles Anthology 1.(Beatles)
THAT'S MY WOMAN	Early Lennon-McCartney piece from Quarry Men days. Played on stage between 1957 and 1959 but never recorded.	
THAT'S WHEN YOUR HEARTACHES BEGIN	Elvis hit from 1957 and included in The Beatles sets from 1959 until 1961 with Paul on lead vocal.	
THINK IT OVER	1958 Buddy Holly song added to The Quarry Men set that year and used through 1962.	
THINKING OF LIKING	One of the earliest Lennon-McCartney pieces from Quarry Men days that was never recorded. Paul always described it as "terrible" and was probably never finished. . Although it may also have been used during the occasional Quarry Men set from 1957 to 1959. There is footage of Paul, George and Ringo performing one (the only ?) verse during their "reunion" session on the Anthology DVD	Beatles Anthology DVD Extras Disc (Beatles)
THREE COOL CATS	Hit for The Coasters in 1959. Included in The Quarry Men set from that year on, first public performance of this song was opening night at The Casbah. Sung by The Beatles during their Decca audition with George on vocals Paul & John on harmony.	Beatles Anthology 1 (Beatles)
THREE STEPS TO HEAVEN	Posthumous hit for Eddie Cochran in 1960 was soon added to The Beatles set.	
TOO BAD ABOUT SORROWS (also TOO MUCH ABOUT SORROWS)	Early McCartney composition from around 1957 included in Quarry Men set, dropped around mid-1959 and never recorded.	
TUTTI FRUITTI	1957 Little Richard hit, added to The Beatles set in early 1960 with Paul on lead.	
TWENTY FLIGHT ROCK	Eddie Cochran song from the movie "The Girl Can't Help It". Included as a part of the early Quarry Men set from October 1957 (?) onwards, part of The Beatles set until 1962.	

WELL (BABY PLEASE DON'T GO)	Recorded by The Olympians, a Los Angeles R&B quartet in 1958 and included in The Beatles set from 1960 to 1962.	
WHAT GOES ON	Lennon tune from "Rubber Soul" that may have been written at this early stage.	Rubber Soul (Beatles)
WHEN	1958 hit for the Kalin Twins and included as part of The Quarry Men set for a short time that year.	
WHEN I'M 64	Originally written by Paul when he was 16 (early 1959) served as the basis for the rewritten version which appeared on Sgt Pepper.	Sgt Pepper's Lonely Hearts Club Band (Beatles)
WHEN THE SAINTS GO MARCHIN IN'	This traditional tune was a included in The Quarry Men sets during 1958 and 1959. Probably due to the influence of the hit "rock" versions from Jerry Lee Lewis (58) and Fats Domino (59)	
WHOLE LOTTA SHAKIN GOIN ON	1957 Jerry Lee Lewis hit. Part of Quarry Men set from 1957 onwards and stayed as part of The Beatles set until 1962.	
WINSTON'S WALK	Early Lennon instrumental piece from Quarry Men days, performed by The Quarry Men on stage between 1957 and 1959 but never recorded.	
WORDS OF LOVE	1957 Buddy Holly song performed by The Quarry Men from 1958 and used through to 1962. One of the rare songs with John and George harmonizing on lead vocal..	
WORRIED MAN BLUES	Lonnie Donegan hit from 1955, also a hit for The vipers in 1957, included in the Quarry Men set from the beginning and used until 1959. Problems transcribing the lyrics from a scratched copy of this record prompted John to start inserting his own word play into songs.	
YEARS ROLL ALONG	Early McCartney piece from Quarry Men days and used on-stage between 1957 and 1959 but never recorded.	
YOU'LL BE MINE	An early Lennon-McCartney composition, captured on the 1960 rehearsal tape. Although there seems to be no record of it being played live.	Beatles Anthology 1 (Beatles)
YOU WERE MEANT FOR ME	Included as part of The Quarry Men set from 1957 until 1960.	
YOU WIN AGAIN	Originally a hit for Hank Williams in 1952 and again for Jerry Lee Lewis in 1958. Added to The Quarry Men set in 58 and used through 1961 with John on lead vocal.	
YOUNGBLOOD	1957 hit for The Coasters and included in The Quarry Men set from 1958 and a regular part of The Beatles set until 1962 with George on lead.	
YOUR TRUE LOVE	Carl Perkins hit from 1957 introduced into The Quarry Men set in 1958 and used through 1962 with George on lead vocal.	

BIBLIOGRAPHY

- Amburn, Ellis. **BUDDY HOLLY: A BIOGRAPHY**. St Martins Press. New York. 1995. ISBN 0-312-13446-0
- Babiuk, Andy. **BEATLES GEAR**. Backbeat Books 2002. San Francisco ISBN 0-87930-731-5
- Baird, Julia. **JOHN LENNON: MY BROTHER**. Grafton 1988. New York. ISBN 0-8050-0793-8
- Beatles. (McCartney, Lennon, Harrison & Starr) **BEATLES ANTHOLOGY**. Chronicle Books. New York. 2000. ISBN 0-81182-6848
- Beatles. **BEATLES ANTHOLOGY**—Video & DVD Series—Apple 1995, 2003—ASIN—B00008GKEG
- Belmo. **NOT FOR SALE: THE BEATLES MUSICAL LEGACY AS ARCHIVED ON UNAUTHORIZED RECORDINGS**. Collectors Guide Publishing. Ontario. ISBN 969-8086-9-7.
- Best, Peter & Doncaster, Patrick. **BEATLE: THE PETE BEST STORY**. Plexus. 1985. London ISBN 0-8596-5077-4
- Best, Roag. **THE BEATLES: THE TRUE BEGINNINGS**. St. Martins Press 2003. New York. ISBN 0-312-31925-8
- Bradman, Keith. **THE BEATLES OFF THE RECORD**. Omnibus Press, 2001. London. ISBN 0-7119-9009-3
- Brown, Peter & Gaines, Stephen. **THE LOVE YOU MAKE: AN INSIDER STORY OF THE BEATLES**. McGraw-Hill. 1983. New York ISBN 0-07-008159
- Buskin, Richard. **THE COMPLETE IDIOTS GUIDE TO . . . THE BEATLES**. Alpha Books. McMillan. New York. 1998 ISBN 0-02-862130-1
- Clayson, Alan. **RINGO STARR: STRAIGHT MAN OR**

- **JOKER**. Sanctuary Publishing. London 1991. ISBN 1-860074-189-4
- Clayson, Alan. **THE QUIET ONE: A LIFE OF GEORGE HARRISON**. Sidgwick & Jackson. 1990. ISBN 1-8607-43498
- Clayson, Alan and Leigh, Spencer. **THE WARLRUS WAS RINGO**. Chrome Dreams 2003. New Malden UK, ISBN 1-84240-205-6
- Coleman, Ray. **LENNON**. McGraw-Hill. New York. 1984. ISBN 0-0609-86085
- Coleman, Ray. **McCARTNEY: YESTERDAY & TODAY**, Boxtree, London. 1995.
- Davies, Hunter. **THE BEATLES AUTHORIZED BIOGRAPHY**. McGraw-Hill. New York 1996 (2nd Edition) ISBN 0-3933-15711
- Davies, Hunter. **THE QUARRYMEN**. Omnibus Press, London 2001, ISBN 0-7119-8526-X
- Davis, Andy. **THE BEATLES FILES**. CLB Publishing 1998. New York. ISBN 1-85833-857-3
- Dowlding, William. **BEATLESONGS**. Fireside 1989. New York. ISBN 0-671-68229-6
- Elliot, Anthony. **THE MOURNING OF JOHN LENNON**. University Of California Press. 1999. Berkeley ISBN 0-520-21549-4
- Epstein, Brian with Taylor Stuart. **A CELLERFULL OF NOISE**. Pocket Books. London 1998 ISBN 0-6710-1196-0
- Everett, Walter. **THE BEATLES AS MUSCIANS: THE QUARRY MEN THROUGH RUBBER SOUL**. Oxford University Press. 2001.New York. ISBN 0-1951-4105-9
- · Fine, Jason (Ed). **HARRISON**. Simon & Shuster, New York 2002, ISBN 0-7432-3581-9.
- Flippo, Chet. **YESTERDAY: THE UNAUTHORIZED BIOGRAPHY OF PAUL McCARTNEY**. Doubleday. New York 1998. ISBN 0-385-23482-1
- Frame, Pete. **THE BEATLES AND SOME OTHER GUYS: ROCK FAMILY TREES OF THE EARLY SIXTIES**. Ominibus. 1997. London ISBN 0-7119-3665-X

- Fulpen, H.V. **THE BEATLES: AN ILLUSTRATED DIARY**. Plexus 1998. London ISBN 0-85965-274-2
- Gambacinni, Paul & Rice, Tim. **GUINESS BOOK OF BRITISH HIT SINGLES**. 7th Edition. Guiness Publishing Ltd. 1989. London. ISBN 0-85112-339-2
- Garry, Len. **JOHN, PAUL & ME: BEFORE THE BEATLES**. CG Publishing. 1997. London. ISBN 0-9695736-8-5
- Geiler, Debbie. **IN MY LIFE: THE BRIAN EPSTEIN STORY**. St. Martins Press 2000. New York. ISBN 0-312-26564-6
- Giuliano, Geoffrey. **TWO OF US: JOHN LENNON & PAUL McCARTNEY—BEHIND THE MYTH**. Penguin 1999. New York. ISBN 0-14-023460-8
- Giuliano, Geoffery. **DARK HORSE: THE LIFE AND ART OF GEORGE HARRISON**. Dutton. 1990. ISBN 0306807475
- Giuliano, Geoffrey. **BLACKBIRD: THE LIFE AND TIMES OF PAUL McCARTNEY**. Penguin. London 1991. ISBN 0-525-93374-3
- Giuliano, Geoffrey. **THE BEATLES, A CELEBRATION**. Thompson Press 1995. London. ISBN 1-85778-000-0
- Goldman, Albert. **THE LIVES OF JOHN LENNON**. William Morrow & Co. New York 1988. ISBN 0-688-04721-1
- Goodrosen, John & Beecher, John. **REMEMBERING BUDDY**. Penguin. New York. 1993. ISBN 0-01401-03635
- Gracen, Jorie. **PAUL McCARTNEY, I SAW HIM STANDING THERE**. Billboard Books 2000. New York ISBN 0-8230-8372-1
- Harry, Bill **THE ENCYLOPEDIA OF BEATLES PEOPLE** Blanford UK 1997. ISBN 0-7137-26067
- Harry, Bill. **THE ULTIMATE BEATLES ENCYCLOPEDIA**. Hyperion. 1992. New York. ISBN 0-7868-8071-6
- Holander, Brock **THE ROCKIN 60s**. Schimer Books / McMillan. New York 1999. ISBN 0-02-864873-0
- Humphries, Patrick. **THE COMPLETE GUIDE TO THE**

MUSIC OF THE BEATLES Vols 1 & 2. Omnibus Press. London. 1998. ISBN 0-7119-6622-2
- Hunt, Chris (ed). **1000 DAYS OF BEALEMANIA: THE EARLY YEARS.** Mojo Special Edition. London. 2002
- Hunt, Chris (ed). **1000 DAYS THAT SHOOK THE WORLD: THE PSYCHEDELIC BEATLES.** Mojo Special Edition. London. 2002
- Kozinn, Allen. **THE BEATLES.** Phaidon 1995. London. ISBN 0-7148-3203-0
- Krebs, Gary. **THE ROCK AND ROLL READER'S GUIDE.** Billboard Books. 1997. New York. ISBN 0-8230-7602-4
- Leach, Sam. **THE BIRTH OF THE BEATLES.** Seven Hills, 1999. ISBN 1-9014-42306
- Lewisohn, Mark **THE COMPLETE BEATLES CHRONICLE,** Hamlyn. 1992 London. ISBN 0-6006-00335
- Mackenzie, Maxwell. **THE BEATLES: EVERY LITTLE THING.** Avon Books Inc. 1998. New York. ISBN 0-380-79698-8
- McDonald, Ian. **REVOLUTION IN THE HEAD: THE BEATLES RECORDS AND THE SIXTIES.** Henry Holt & Co. New York. 1994—ISBN 0-8050-2780-7
- Miles, Barry. **JOHN LENNON: IN HIS OWN WORDS.** Omnibus Press. London. 1980. ISBN 0-86001-816-4
- Miles, Barry. **PAUL McCARTNEY: MANY YEARS FROM NOW.** Henry Holt & Co. New York 1997. ISBN 0-8050-5248-8.
- Miles, Barry. **THE BEATLES—A DIARY.** Omnibus Press. 1998.—ISBN 0-7119-6315-0
- Norman, Philip. **SHOUT: THE BEATLES IN THEIR GENERATION.** MJF Books. 1981. New York. ISBN 1-56731-087-7
- Palmer, Robert. **ROCK & ROLL: AN UNRULY HISTORY.** Harmony Books. 1995. New York. ISBN 0-517=70050-6

- Pawlowski, Garth L. **HOW THEY BECAME THE BEATLES—A DEFINITIVE HISTORY OF THE EARLY YEARS 1960-64.** Dutton. New York 1989. ISBN 0-525-24823-4
- Pritchard, David & Lysaght, Alan. **THE BEATLES: AN ORAL HISTORY.** Hyperion 1998. New York. ISBN 0-7868-6436-2
- Robertson, John. **LENNON: A JOURNEY THROUGH JOHN LENNON'S LIFE & TIMES IN WORDS & PICTURES.** Omnibus Press. London. 1995. ISBN 0-7119-4981-6
- Robertson, John. **THE ART & MUSIC OF JOHN LENNON.** Carol Publishing. 1991. New York. ISBN 1-55972-076-X
- Rolling Stone, (Ed) **HARRISON.** Simon & Schuster. New York, 2002. ISBN 0-74323-5819
- Rosen, Robert. **NOWHERE MAN: THE FINAL DAYS OF JOHN LENNON.** Soft Skull Press Inc. 2000. New York.
- Shapiro, Marc. **BEHIND SAD EYES: THE LIFE OF GEORGE HARRISON**, St. Martin's Press, 2002, New York. ISBN 0-312-30109-X
- Spignesi, Stephen **THE BEATLES BOOK OF LISTS**, Citadel Press, Secaucus NJ. 1998. ISBN 0-8065-1972
- Sutcliffe, Pauline & Thompson, Douglas. **THE BEATLES SHADOW: STUART SUTCLIFFE & HIS LONELY HEARTS CLUB.** Sidwick & Jackson, London 2001. ISBN 0-283-07342-X
- Sutherland, Steve (Ed). **NME ORIGINALS: THE BEATLES.** IPC Ignite, London , 2001.
- Thompson, Dave. **BETTER TO BURN OUT: THE CULT OF DEATH IN ROCK N ROLL.** Thunders Mouth Press. 1999. New York. ISBN 1-56025-1905. (Discusses John Lennon and Stuart Sutcliffe)
- Turner, Steve. **A HARD DAY'S WRITE.** HarperCollins. New York 1994 ISBN 0-06-095065-X

- Various. **BEATLES DIGEST.** 2nd Edition. Krause Publications 2002. ISBN 0-87349-512-8
- Various. **THE DAY THE MUSIC DIED: A ROCK N ROLL TRIBUTE.** Plexus, London. 1994. ISBN 0859650588 (John Lennon discussed).
- Venezia, Mike. **GETTING TO KNOW THE WORLD'S GREATEST COMPOSERS: THE BEATLES,** Grolier, New York—1997, ISBN: 0-516-20310
- Wiener, Jon. **COME TOGETHER: JOHN LENNON IN HIS TIME.**, University of Illinois, 1991 ISBN 0571135765
- Zimmer, Dave. **CROSBY, STILLS & NASH.** DeCapo Press 2000. New York. ISBN 0-306-80974-5

MAGAZINES

- ❖ **BEATLOLOGY MAGAZINE**—Inhouse productions—ISSN 1488-1381
- ❖ **CLASSIC ROCK**—Future Publishing
- ❖ **ENTERTAINMENT WEEKLY**—Time Inc.
- ❖ **GOOD DAY SUNSHINE**—GDS Publications—ISSN 1041-4118
- ❖ **GUITAR ONE**—Cherry Lane Magazines
- ❖ **GUITAR PLAYER**—Music Player Publications
- ❖ **GUITAR WORLD**—Guitar World Magazine
- ❖ **MOJO**—EMAP Metro Ltd
- ❖ **NEW MUSICAL EXPRESS**—IPC Magazines
- ❖ **Q**—EMAP Metro Ltd
- ❖ **ROLLING STONE**—Wenner Media LLC
- ❖ **THE BEATLES BOOK**—Beat Publications Ltd.

WEBSITES

- ❖ *Official Beatles site*—http://thebeatles.com
- ❖ *Beatle Fest—Conventions and Memorabilia*—http://www.thefestforbeatlesfans.com

- *Beatle Links—The Beatles Internet Resource Guide*—http://www.beatlelinks.net
- *The Quarrymen—official website of the re-formed Quarrymen*—http://www.quarrymen.co.uk/

REFERENCES

1. New Groves Dictionary Of Music
2. From Davies, THE QUARRYMEN.
3. Ibid.
4. Correspondence from Rod Davis to the author.
5. John Lennon on BEATLES ANTHOLOGY Video Vol. 1.
6. Correspondence from Rod Davis to author.
7. From "Close-up on a Beatle" interview with Alan Smith, NEW MUSICAL EXPRESS, 30 August 1963.
8. Goldman. THE LIVES OF JOHN LENNON.
9. Davies. THE QUARRYMEN
10. Correspondence from Rod Davis to author.
11. Goldman. THE LIVES OF JOHN LENNON.
12. John Lennon quoted in Goldman's THE LIVES OF JOHN LENNON
13. George from BEATLES ANTHOLOGY Video Vol. 1.
14. George from BEATLES ANTHOLOGY Video Vol. 1.
15. Shapiro. BEHIND SAD EYES: THE LIFE OF GEORGE HARRISON,
16. Paul on BEATLES ANTHOLOGY Video Vol. 1.
17. George on BEATLES ANTHOLOGY Video Vol. 1.
18. Miles. PAUL McCARTNEY: MANY YEARS FROM NOW
19. Clayson, Alan. RINGO STARR: STRAIGHT MAN OR JOKER
20. Miles. JOHN LENNON: IN HIS OWN WORDS.
21. The following sources all give the date of the founding of The Quarry Men as March 1957:
    -Miles. THE BEATLES—A DIARY.
    -Norman. SHOUT: THE BEATLES IN THEIR GENERATION
    -Buskin. THE COMPLETE IDIOTS GUIDE TO… THE BEATLES.

The following sources give the date as an unspecified month in 1956
    -Holander. THE ROCKIN 60s.
    -Palmer. ROCK & ROLL: AN UNRULY HISTORY.

22	Correspondence from Rod Davis to author.
23	Garry. JOHN, PAUL & ME: BEFORE THE BEATLES.
24	Ibid
25	Correspondence from Rod Davis to author.
26	Colin Hanton quoted in Davies, THE QUARRYMEN.
27	Correspondence from Rod Davis to author.
28	Ibid. Other sources quote the relevant line from the school song as "*Quarrymen strong before our birth.*" But I have taken the quote as supplied directly by one of the few original participants who was also a student at the school and present at the time of the naming of the group.
29	Davies, THE QUARRYMEN.
30	Correspondence from Rod Davis to author.
31	Turner. A HARD DAY'S WRITE.
32	Guliano. BLACKBIRD: THE LIFE AND TIMES OF PAUL McCARTNEY.
33	Some sources (notably 1000 DAYS OF BEATLEMANIA) give the date of the concert as 11th November.
34	Date given by Rod Davis in correspondence with the author, taken from postcard of the bill for the show. Giuliano in TWO OF US: JOHN LENNON & PAUL McCARTNEY—BEHIND THE MYTH. Places the concert as the 11th November Interestingly Guilano gives the date as 1958 in his earlier George Harrison biography (DARK HORSE: THE LIFE AND ART OF GEORGE HARRISON), but considering that the skiffle craze was over by late 1957 this later date is unlikely. Harry in his THE ULTIMATE BEATLES ENCYCLOPEDIA indicates that Paul McCartney was 14 at the time, so this places the concert date between July 1956 and July 1957.
35	"Cavern Girl" Liz Huges in Pritchard & Lysaght. THE BEATLES: AN ORAL HISTORY.
36	ibid
37	Davies, THE QUARRYMEN
38	Ibid.
39	Pritchard & Lysaght. THE BEATLES: AN ORAL HISTORY.
40	Correspondence from Rod Davis to author.
41	Guilano. DARK HORSE: THE LIFE AND ART OF GEORGE HARRISON.

42. Correspondence from Rod Davis to author.
43. Charlie Roberts quoted in Goldman. THE LIVES OF JOHN LENNON.
44. Harry. THE ULTIMATE BEATLES ENCYCLOPEDIA.
45. Baird. JOHN LENNON: MY BROTHER.
46. Correspondence from Rod Davis to author.
47. Quoted in Davies, THE QUARRYMEN.
48. Giuliano. TWO OF US: JOHN LENNON & PAUL McCARTNEY—BEHIND THE MYTH. and in BLACKBIRD: THE LIFE AND TIMES OF PAUL McCARTNEY.
49. Paul McCartney interviewed on PARKINSON—BBC TV 2000.
50. Buskin. THE COMPLETE IDIOTS GUIDE TO… THE BEATLES.
51. Norman. SHOUT: THE BEATLES IN THEIR GENERATION.
52. Garry. JOHN, PAUL & ME: BEFORE THE BEATLES.
53. Ibid
54. Mimi Smith quoted in Goldman. THE LIVES OF JOHN LENNON.
55. Norman. SHOUT: THE BEATLES IN THEIR GENERATION.
56. Paul on BEATLES ANTHOLOGY video Vol. 1
57. Garry. JOHN, PAUL & ME: BEFORE THE BEATLES.
58. "One of the group lent me his guitar."—Paul interviewed on PARKINSON, BBC TV 2000.
59. Correspondence from Rod Davis to author.
60. Guliano. BLACKBIRD: THE LIFE AND TIMES OF PAUL McCARTNEY.
61. Garry. JOHN, PAUL & ME: BEFORE THE BEATLES.
62. Buskin. THE COMPLETE IDIOTS GUIDE TO… THE BEATLES.
63. John on BEATLES ANTHOLOGY Video Vol. 1.
64. From Buskin, Garry and Giullano
65. Correspondence from Rod Davis to author.
66. Robertson,. LENNON: A JOURNEY THROUGH JOHN LENNON'S LIFE & TIMES IN WORDS & PICTURES.
67. Quoted in 1000 DAYS OF BEATLEMANIA.
68. Harry. THE ULTIMATE BEATLES ENCYCLOPEDIA. and Guliano BLACKBIRD: THE LIFE AND TIMES OF PAUL McCARTNEY.
69. Miles. THE BEATLES—A DIARY. Omnibus Press.
70. Correspondence from Rod Davis to author.
71. Sutcliffe & Thompson. THE BEATLES SHADOW
72. ibid.

73 ibid.
74 Guliano. BLACKBIRD: THE LIFE AND TIMES OF PAUL McCARTNEY.
75 Paul interviewed on PARKINSON, BBC TV—2000.
76 Pritchard & Lysaght,. THE BEATLES: AN ORAL HISTORY.
77 Turner. A HARD DAY'S WRITE.
78 Sutcliffe & Thompson ,THE BEATLES SHADOW
79 Some sources (notably Spignesi in THE BEATLES LISTS) document George's first attendance at a Quarry Men gig as the February 6, 1958 show at the Wilson Hall. Other sources point to this date of December 7, 1957 and as it seems to fit the flow of events better I have selected to conform with the majority viewpoint.
80 Quoted in Davies, THE QUARRYMEN.
81 Correspondence from Rod Davis to author.
82 Paul on BEATLES ANTHOLOGY Video Vol. 1
83 Amburn. BUDDY HOLLY: A BIOGRAPHY.
84 ibid
85 Paul on BEATLES ANTHOLOGY Video Vol. 1.
86 Amburn. BUDDY HOLLY: A BIOGRAPHY.
87 Shapiro. BEHIND SAD EYES: THE LIFE OF GEORGE HARRISON,
88 Elliot. THE MOURNING OF JOHN LENNON.
89 Harry. THE ULTIMATE BEATLES ENCYCLOPEDIA.
90 Correspondence from Rod Davis to author.
91 Ibid
92 Harry. THE ULTIMATE BEATLES ENCYCLOPEDIA.
93 Brown & Gaines. THE LOVE YOU MAKE: AN INSIDER STORY OF THE BEATLES.
94 Pawlowski. HOW THEY BECAME THE BEATLES—A DEFINITIVE HISTORY OF THE EARLY YEARS 1960-64.
95 Goldman. THE LIVES OF JOHN LENNON.
96 Pawlowski. HOW THEY BECAME THE BEATLES—A DEFINITIVE HISTORY OF THE EARLY YEARS 1960-64.
97 Fulpen. THE BEATLES: AN ILLUSTRATED DIARY.
98 From "Close-up on a Beatle" interview by Alan Smith, NEW MUSICAL EXPRESS, 9th August 1963.
99 Epstein with Taylor. A CELLERFULL OF NOISE.

100. Garry. JOHN, PAUL & ME: BEFORE THE BEATLES.
101. Paul on BEATLES ANTHOLOGY Video Vol. 1.
102. From "Close up on a Beatle" interview with Alan Smith. NEW MUSICAL EXPRESS 16th August 1963.
103. Clayson, THE QUIET ONE
104. From "Close-up on a Beatle" interview with Alan Smith, NEW MUSICAL EXPRESS 23 August 1963.
105. Pritchard & Lysaght. THE BEATLES: AN ORAL HISTORY.
106. Best & Doncaster. BEATLE: THE PETE BEST STORY.
107. Ibid
108. Ibid
109. As quoted in Harry. THE ULTIMATE BEATLES ENCYCLOPEDIA.
110. Pawlowski. HOW THEY BECAME THE BEATLES—A DEFINITIVE HISTORY OF THE EARLY YEARS 1960-64.
111. Harry. THE ULTIMATE BEATLES ENCYCLOPEDIA
112. Paul on BEATLES ANTHOLOGY Video Vol. 1.
113. Buskin. THE COMPLETE IDIOTS GUIDE TO… THE BEATLES.
114. Sutcliffe & Thompson. THE BEATLES SHADOW
115. George on BEATLES ANTHOLOGY Video Vol. 1
116. Harry. THE ULTIMATE BEATLES ENCYCLOPEDIA
117. Pritchard, & Lysaght. THE BEATLES: AN ORAL HISTORY.
118. Harry. THE ULTIMATE BEATLES ENCYCLOPEDIA.
119. Sutcliffe & Thompson. THE BEATLES SHADOW
120. Pritchard & Lysaght. THE BEATLES: AN ORAL HISTORY.
121. quoted from Spignesi THE BEATLES BOOK OF LISTS,
122. Goodrosen & Beecher. REMEMBERING BUDDY.
123. Reproduced in Sutcliffe & Thompson. THE BEATLES SHADOW
124. Paul on BEATLES ANTHOLOGY Video Vol. 1.
125. Clayson, RINGO STARR, STRAIGHT MAN OR JOKER?
126. Pawlowski. HOW THEY BECAME THE BEATLES—A DEFINITIVE HISTORY OF THE EARLY YEARS 1960-64.
127. Fulpen. THE BEATLES: AN ILLUSTRATED DIARY.
128. Paul on BEATLES ANTHOLOGY Video Vol. 1.
129. Harry. THE ULTIMATE BEATLES ENCYCLOPEDIA.
130. ibid
131. ibid

132. Sutcliffe & Thompson. THE BEATLES SHADOW
133. As recalled by Paul in "Close-up on a Beatle" interview with Alan Smith, NEW MUSICAL EXPRESS, 9 August 1963.
134. Harry. THE ULTIMATE BEATLES ENCYCLOPEDIA.
135. Guliano,. BLACKBIRD: THE LIFE AND TIMES OF PAUL McCARTNEY.
136. George on BEATLES ANTHOLOGY Vol. 1.
137. Harry. THE ULTIMATE BEATLES ENCYCLOPEDIA.
138. Guilano. DARK HORSE: THE LIFE AND ART OF GEORGE HARRISON.
139. Harry. THE ULTIMATE BEATLES ENCYCLOPEDIA.
140. Brown, & Gaines. THE LOVE YOU MAKE: AN INSIDER STORY OF THE BEATLES.
141. Pritchard & Lysaght. THE BEATLES: AN ORAL HISTORY.
142. Harry. THE ULTIMATE BEATLES ENCYCLOPEDIA.
143. George on BEATLES ANTHOLOGY Video Vol. 1.
144. Best & Doncaster. BEATLE: THE PETE BEST STORY.
145. Pritchard & Lysaght. THE BEATLES: AN ORAL HISTORY.
146. ibid

www.ingramcontent.com/pod-product-compliance
Lightning Source LLC
Chambersburg PA
CBHW022105160426
43198CB00008B/359